Discovery Assessments

How to Challenge Them

4th Edition

Keith Gordon

Law date

The text is based on the tax law as at 1 October 2023.

1st edition January 2017
This 4th edition November 2023

www.carbonbalancedprint.com
CBP2250

The carbon emissions of the paper used to produce this book have been offset via the World Land Trust's Carbon Balanced Paper scheme.

This product is made of material from well-managed, FSC®-certified forests and other controlled sources.

Discovery Assessments

How to Challenge Them

4th Edition

Keith Gordon

Published by:

Claritax Books Ltd
6 Grosvenor Park Road
Chester, CH1 1QQ

www.claritaxbooks.com

ISBN: 978-1-912386-91-8

Tax titles from Claritax Books

General tax annuals

- Capital Gains Tax
- Income Tax
- Inheritance Tax
- National Insurance Contributions
- Stamp Duty Land Tax
- Value Added Tax

Specialist tax annuals

- Advising British Expats
- A-Z of Plant & Machinery
- Capital Allowances
- Financial Planning with Trusts
- Pension Tax Guide
- Property Investment

Other specialist titles

- Construction Industry Scheme
- Cryptocurrency and Other Digital Assets
- Discovery Assessments
- Disguised Remuneration
- Employee Share Schemes
- Employee-Ownership Trusts
- Employment Status
- Enterprise Investment Scheme
- Furnished Holiday Lettings
- Living and Working Abroad
- Main Residence Relief
- Personal Representatives
- Research and Development
- Residence: The Definition in Practice
- Schedule 36 Notices
- Tax Appeals
- Tax Losses
- Taxation of Partnerships
- Taxpayer Safeguards

See www.claritaxbooks.com for details of all our titles.

About the author

Keith M Gordon MA (Oxon), FCA, CTA (Fellow), Barrister practises from Temple Tax Chambers in London. He previously worked as a chartered accountant and chartered tax adviser. His practice covers all areas of tax, and also related areas including partnership disputes and professional negligence. He regularly appears in the tax tribunals and the higher courts.

Keith lectures and writes extensively and won the "tax writer of the year" category in the 2013 LexisNexis Taxation awards, having been a runner-up in 2006 and 2012. In 2009, Keith won the "CTA of the year" category and in 2019 he won the award for "outstanding contribution to tax".

Keith's recent cases include the IR35 cases of *Albatel* (at the FTT), *Red White and Green* (at the Upper Tribunal) and *Atholl House* (at the Upper Tribunal and Court of Appeal). He was also junior Counsel for the taxpayer in *Jones v Garnett* (the "Arctic Systems" case) in the Court of Appeal and the House of Lords. He has also acted for the taxpayer in many of the leading cases on discovery assessments, in particular in *Charlton, Pattullo, Sanderson, Hicks, Atherton* and *Anderson.*

FOR MY DAUGHTER, SARAH

Preface

I am delighted to have had the opportunity to update this book.

As I have noted in the preface to the previous editions, the topic of discovery assessments has been of considerable interest to me for what is now two decades. In those early days, it was very much a "minority interest" sport and I remember appearing in tribunals and having to explain carefully the purpose and structure of the discovery provisions. Now, the rules represent a staple food within the tribunals' diet as the number of cases will testify.

The main event of the previous edition was the Supreme Court's decision in the *Tooth* case. The ongoing repercussions of that case are still being litigated and the developments so far are reflected in this edition.

The big case to feature in this edition is the Court of Appeal's decision in *Wilkes*. Although perhaps not quite as ground-breaking as *Tooth*, the *Wilkes* case did achieve something not achieved in *Tooth* – that was to prompt a change in the legislation itself. Indeed, the government felt it needed to protect itself by ensuring that the change of the law should be applied retroactively. The new statutory rules are thus considered in this edition, together with a discussion of how the old rules continue to operate in certain limited cases.

Other than that, there has been a steady stream of cases consolidating the law in respect of most aspects of the discovery rules. Changes for this edition therefore include:

- *Wilkes* comment on TMA 1970, s. 29 since introduction of self-assessment (**2.1.2**);
- concept of "relevant discovery" (**3.1**);
- *Marano* re need for HMRC functions to be carried out by human agency (**3.2.1**);
- *Wilkes* ruling that the subject matter of the discovery assessment must relate to the underlying discovery (**3.3.1**);
- FA 2022 removal of anomaly re tax that "ought" to have been assessed (**3.3.1** and **3.8.4**);

- *Islam* case re need for HMRC to use reasonable methods to demonstrate that there has been a discovery (**3.3.7**);
- *Wilby* SDLT case re mismatch of information justifying a discovery assessment (**3.3.7**);
- Upper Tribunal *Norton* comment on need to determine an assessment's procedural validity at the time the assessment is made (**3.5.2**);
- discussion of whether a discovery assessment may be made during an enquiry window (**3.5.2**);
- corporation tax powers re surplus dual inclusion income (**3.6.1**);
- discovery provisions for digital services tax (**3.7.3**), public interest business protection tax (**3.7.4**) and multinational top-up tax (**3.7.5**);
- *Ashe* case re limits of retrospective legislation (**3.8.6**);
- *Kensall* re HMRC misinformation about prospects of appeal (**3.8.6**);
- resolution of further "staleness" cases following Supreme Court ruling in *Tooth* (**3.9.5**);
- a new **Chapter 4** has been inserted (and later numbering adjusted accordingly) re additional taxpayer safeguards when a return has been made;
- additional safeguards for other taxes (corporation tax, SDLT, ATED, digital services tax, public interest business protection tax, multinational top-up tax) (**4.3**);
- Upper Tribunal *Hargreaves* case re carelessness not necessarily justifying a discovery assessment (**5.3.1**);
- *McCumiskey* and *Robson* cases re returns made by fraudulent advisers without proper taxpayer authorisation (**5.3.2**);
- *Robson* draws distinction between carelessness and fraudulent conduct (**5.3.3**; also **5.5.1**);
- discussion of principle of careless conduct having to cause loss of tax (*Bella Figura* and *Delphi*) (**5.4.3**);
- further case law discussing carelessness in practice (including *Kingdon*, *Rizvi* and *Altunis*) (**5.4.4**);

- *CPR* case re submission of document where taxpayer suspects it is inaccurate (**5.5.4**);
- further case law discussion of deliberate inaccuracies, including *Quinns* and *Arthur* (**5.5.6**);
- careless or deliberate behaviour in context of digital services tax (**5.6.4**), public interest business protection tax (**5.6.5**) and multinational top-up tax (**5.6.6**);
- *Buckingham* discussion re meaning of "enquiry" in context of discovery assessments (**6.5.3**);
- *McCumiskey* and *Sheth* cases re imputation of information to hypothetical officer (**6.5.4**), and discussion of officer awareness of insufficiency (**6.6**);
- *Hargreaves* discussion re prevailing practice (**7.2.4**);
- defences against discovery assessments in context of digital services tax (**7.3.4**), public interest business protection tax (**7.3.5**) and multinational top-up tax (**7.3.6**);
- *Mullens* case re HMRC only needing to show careless conduct if assessment within time limits (**8.2.3** and **8.2.4**);
- failure to notify chargeability (including HICBC) and *Hextall* case re meaning of reasonable excuse (**8.2.4**);
- *Scott* case re extended time limits for offshore assessments (**8.4.2**);
- time limits for discovery assessments in context of digital services tax (**8.5.4**), public interest business protection tax (**8.5.5**) and multinational top-up tax (**8.5.6**);
- *Wilby* confirmation that FTT does not necessarily have to be able to identify the officer who made the discovery (but that should be rare) (**9.1.1**);
- Upper Tribunal *Birkett* case dilutes principle that FTT may never consider arguments that would normally be considered under judicial review procedures (**9.2.2**);
- further case law discussions re burden of proof in discovery cases, including *Kingdon* and *Hargreaves* (**9.3.3**);
- problematic *Civic* case re supplementary claims (**10.3.3**) and re claims affecting more than one period (**10.7.4**);

- consequential claims in relation to SDLT, ATED and certain other taxes (**10.8**); and

- interaction between discovery assessments and investigatory powers for digital services tax, public interest business protection tax and multinational top-up tax (**11.3**).

This publication would not have been possible without the ongoing practical support of Ray Chidell at Claritax Books. Similarly, I am grateful for the unfailing support of my wife and daughter.

I would also like to acknowledge the helpful comments received from one reader, Julian Maples, which I hope I have fully reflected in this edition.

Finally, as was the case in earlier editions, I cannot end this preface without recording my continued appreciation of the late and much-missed Andy Wells. Many parts of this book (as with much of my early work on the subject of discovery assessments) have greatly benefited from Andy's wise counsel. Any errors, needless to say, are my own.

Keith M Gordon
Temple Tax Chambers

October 2023

Abbreviations

APN	Accelerated payment notice
Art.	Article
ATED	Annual tax on enveloped dwellings
CGT	Capital gains tax
CH	Compliance Handbook
CIS	Construction Industry Scheme
CRCA 2005	Commissioners for Revenue and Customs Act 2005
CSOH	Court of Session Outer House
CTSA	Corporation tax self-assessment
DOTAS	Disclosure of tax avoidance schemes
EWCA	England and Wales Court of Appeal
EWHC	England and Wales High Court
FA	Finance Act
FTT	First-tier Tribunal
HICBC	High income child benefit charge
HMRC	HM Revenue and Customs
ITA 2007	Income Tax Act 2007
ITEPA 2003	Income Tax (Earnings and Pensions) Act 2003
ITSA	Income tax self-assessment
J	Mr or Mrs Justice
LJ	Lord or Lady Justice
LLP	Limited liability partnership
MTD	Making Tax Digital
Oao	On the application of
Para.	Paragraph
POTAS	Promoters of tax avoidance schemes
PPN	Partner payment notice
S.	Section
SACM	Self Assessment Claims Manual
Sch.	Schedule
SDLT	Stamp duty land tax
SI	Statutory instrument
SP	Statement of practice
Sp C	Special Commissioners
T/a	Trading as
TC	Tax Chamber
TCC	Tax and Chancery Chamber
TCGA 1992	Taxation of Chargeable Gains Act 1992
TMA 1970	Taxes Management Act 1970
UKFTT	United Kingdom First-tier Tribunal

UKSC	United Kingdom Supreme Court
UKUT	United Kingdom Upper Tribunal
VAT	Value added tax

Table of contents

1.   Overview of the book

This book guides the reader through the various issues relating to discovery assessments.

The book focuses on the rules as they apply to income tax and capital gains tax (CGT), but then considers the variants to these rules so far as other taxes are concerned.

In short, the book covers:

- the various conditions for making a discovery assessment;
- how discovery assessments may be challenged;
- consequential claims by taxpayers in light of a discovery assessment; and
- the relationship between discovery assessments and HMRC's investigatory powers.

2.   Introduction to discovery assessments

2.1   Introduction

2.1.1   *Historical context*

The former Inland Revenue (now HMRC) long had a power to issue assessments upon discovering that taxpayers had paid too little tax. That power was not abolished when self-assessment was introduced (with effect from 6 April 1996).

Nevertheless, self-assessment provides HMRC with additional powers to review what taxpayers have done in their tax returns, most notably with the right to open a statutory enquiry (usually) within twelve months of the tax return being submitted. Once an enquiry is opened, HMRC have no statutory time limit for bringing it to a conclusion, although taxpayers have a right to ask the tribunal to direct that an enquiry be closed within a specified period, a power that the tribunal must exercise unless it considers that HMRC have good reason to continue their investigations.

Law: TMA 1970, s. 28A(4), (6)

2.1.2   *Relationship with self-assessment*

However, the additional burdens imposed on taxpayers under self-assessment led Parliament to limit the situations in which a taxpayer may be subjected to a discovery assessment. As the Court of Appeal held in *Tower MCashback* (and as was later endorsed by the Supreme Court in *Tooth*):

> "[Apart from the specific interventions permitted under the self assessment rules themselves,] the only other method by which the Revenue can impose additional tax liabilities or recover excessive reliefs is under the new s. 29. That confers a far more restricted power than that contained in the previous s. 29. ... These provisions underline the finality of the self-assessment, a finality which is underlined by strict statutory control of the circumstances in which the Revenue may impose additional tax liabilities by way of amendment to the taxpayer's return and assessment."

More recently, the Court of Appeal in *Wilkes* noted that "once self-assessment had been introduced, section 29 [of TMA 1970] was in general terms meant to provide a back-up to that [i.e. the taxpayer's self-assessment process] as well as to assessment by HMRC [which is understood to mean HMRC's power of amendment following an enquiry]".

Accordingly, discovery assessments represent HMRC's residual power to be used when the standard enquiry procedures could not reasonably have been used by HMRC in any particular case.

However, it must be remembered that different taxes have slightly different enquiry procedures which should not be overlooked. For example, for corporation tax, not only are HMRC entitled to amend tax returns via closure notices, but they are also entitled to make consequential amendments in respect of tax returns not under enquiry.

Example 1

Ollie Ltd claimed a capital loss of £1m in its return for the year to 31 December 2023, of which £400,000 was used in the year and £600,000 carried forward to, and used in, the following year.

At the conclusion of an enquiry into the 2023 return, HMRC could remove the loss in its entirety and consequentially amend the 2024 return to reflect their view that there should be no loss brought forward from the previous year.

However, the author has seen HMRC try to use consequential amendments in circumstances outside those prescribed by the statute, claiming that they wish to reflect the view formed in the enquiry year in all returns where a similar issue arises.

Example 2

Archie Ltd incurred expenditure in 2023 and 2024 which it treated as qualifying for a revenue deduction in its returns for the two years ended 31 December 2023 and 2024. HMRC opened an enquiry into the 2023 return, but not the 2024 return.

When concluding the enquiry, HMRC took the view that the expense was capital in nature. They can amend the 2023 return when issuing the closure notice. But they may not make a consequential amendment to the 2024 return. Any adjustment to 2024 has to be by way of discovery assessment (subject to all the statutory conditions being met).

For example, in *Steadfast*, the reasons for the withdrawal of the consequential amendment are not disclosed. However, the tribunal noted that the adjustment sought by HMRC should have been by way of a discovery assessment.

Law: FA 1998, Sch. 18, para. 34(2A)

Cases: *Tower MCashback LLP v HMRC* [2010] EWCA Civ 32; *Steadfast Manufacturing & Storage Ltd v HMRC* [2020] UKFTT 286 (TC); *HMRC v Tooth* [2021] UKSC 17; *HMRC v Wilkes* [2022] EWCA Civ 1612

2.2 Discovery assessments in practice

2.2.1 *When discovery assessments arise*

In the theoretical world, a discovery assessment is most likely to arise as a result of a self-assessment enquiry into a taxpayer in the course of which an error is identified. If HMRC have reason to believe that that the same (or a similar) error is likely to have occurred in another tax year, HMRC may well make a discovery assessment in respect of that other year.

There will also be situations in which HMRC newly come across information (for example, a tip-off from a former spouse or employee) that alerts them to a historical under-assessment. In such situations, assuming that the subsequent investigation confirms the under-assessment, a discovery assessment is likely to be appropriate.

Discovery assessments can also arise when HMRC (either as a result of legal developments elsewhere or simply a genuine change of interpretation) consider that the law gives rise to a different outcome from that previously thought to be the case.

Finally (and worryingly commonly) there are situations in which HMRC have simply failed to open an enquiry in time (even in cases in which they were already investigating a taxpayer in respect of other years). In such cases, HMRC's only way of collecting any additional tax now thought to be due is by making a discovery assessment. It is in such cases that the statutory safeguards (which should never be overlooked) are most likely to come to the taxpayer's aid.

2.2.2   Dealing with a discovery assessment

In each case, although HMRC might well have identified tax that should have been assessed, in order to secure that additional tax, HMRC have to demonstrate that the additional statutory conditions for a discovery assessment are met.

Indeed, most of the leading cases concerning discovery assessments have not involved any dispute as to the amount of tax that should have been paid: instead, the only dispute was whether the discovery assessment rules meant that the tax could still be demanded.

The discovery assessment rules, therefore, are a type of statutory limitation, peculiar to the tax code. In the same way as an individual should not hesitate to argue that a 20-year old debt (for example) is statute-barred, there is no reason why a taxpayer should not argue that the statutory rules governing discovery assessments preclude HMRC from collecting a particular sum now thought to be payable. Indeed, in *Abdulla*, the Supreme Court has provided a reminder of the validity of such arguments:

> "... issues of limitation are bedevilled by an unarticulated tendency to treat it as an unmeritorious procedural technicality. This is, I think, unjustified. Limitation in English law is generally procedural. But it is not a technicality, nor is it necessarily unmeritorious. It has been part of English statute law for nearly four centuries. It has generated analogous non-statutory principles in equity. Some form of limitation is a feature of almost all other systems of law. And it has been accepted in principle in the jurisprudence of both the Court of Justice of the European Union and the European Court of Human Rights. Limitation reflects a fundamental and all but universal legal policy that the litigation of stale claims is potentially a significant injustice. Delay impoverishes the evidence available to determine the claim, prolongs uncertainty, impedes the definitive settlement of the parties' mutual affairs and consumes scarce judicial resources in dealing with claims that should have been brought long ago or not at all."

Case: *Birmingham City Council v Abdulla* [2012] UKSC 47

5

2.2.3   HMRC's approach to discovery assessments

In practice, however, HMRC often treat discovery assessments as simply another way of collecting tax that they consider to be due and pay little regard to the statutory hurdles that need to be overcome in such cases. Even when they are themselves aware of the restrictions, they sometimes fail to make it clear to taxpayers (or their advisers) how HMRC consider the statutory conditions to be met.

Consequently, many taxpayers will read HMRC's correspondence and take it at face value without realising that a viable defence is available to them.

Example

HMRC write to Jake to alert him to an under-assessment seven years ago. They carefully explain why they believe that tax has been under-assessed, but fail to explain why they consider a discovery assessment will be valid.

Since discovery assessments (particularly going back more than four years) are subject to additional conditions (which HMRC are obliged to satisfy), HMRC's silence might lull Jake into thinking that the additional tax should be paid.

Had HMRC told Jake that they also needed to prove that the under-assessment was deliberate, and had they also attempted to explain why they considered that to be the case, Jake might then be in a position to counter HMRC's claim.

The Upper Tribunal's decision in *Burgess/Brimheath* should level things up slightly because it requires HMRC, at the tribunal, to prove that each condition for a discovery assessment is indeed satisfied. However, most cases do not find their way to the tribunal, meaning that it is incumbent on taxpayers or their advisers to ensure that HMRC stick to the rules. See also **9.4**.

Case: *Burgess v HMRC, Brimheath Developments Ltd v HMRC* [2015] UKUT 578 (TCC)

2.3 The ingredients of a discovery assessment

2.3.1 The basic conditions

In all cases, HMRC must first show that they have "discovered" an earlier under-assessment. This is the test that long pre-dated the self-assessment rules. This requirement is discussed in **Chapter 3**.

Secondly (assuming that the taxpayer had filed a return for the relevant period), the changes introduced by self-assessment require HMRC to show, in addition, that they can overcome one (or both) of the following two hurdles:

- that the original under-assessment was attributable to the careless or deliberate conduct of the taxpayer (or a person acting on the taxpayer's behalf) (discussed in **Chapter 5**); or

- that the tax return (and other documentation deemed to be before a "hypothetical tax officer") would not have been sufficient to alert the hypothetical officer to the under-assessment (discussed in **Chapter 6**).

It must be emphasised that the second set of safeguards does not apply to taxpayers who have not submitted a tax return for the relevant tax year. In those cases, the only procedural hurdle that HMRC generally need to overcome is to show that they have made a discovery.

2.3.2 Time limits

In some cases, however, HMRC do have a further obstacle to overcome: statutory time limits.

Unlike closure notices in the case of self-assessment enquiries, the statute imposes time limits on the issue of discovery assessments. HMRC are also required to demonstrate that these time limits have not been breached.

The time limits are discussed in **Chapter 8.**

2.4 A statutory defence against a discovery assessment

Finally, the statute provides a further opportunity for a discovery assessment to be challenged. To do so, the taxpayer must be able to demonstrate that the original return (containing the under-assessment) was prepared in accordance with the then prevailing practice.

This defence is discussed further in **Chapter 7.**

2.5   HMRC Statements of Practice

For completeness, it should be noted that the former Inland Revenue and HMRC published two Statements of Practice which govern what is now HMRC's approach to discovery assessments (SP 8/91 and SP 1/06). The first is nowadays of mainly historical relevance and focuses on the right of HMRC to make a discovery assessment in cases where a prior agreement has been reached between them and a taxpayer on a particular matter. The second represents HMRC's views on when HMRC can make a discovery assessment where information has previously been provided to HMRC but where there has not necessarily been any prior agreement by an officer.

These Statements of Practice are both rather out of date and of limited practical value. However, their text is analysed in **Appendix 1** and **Appendix 2**.

Guidance: HMRC Statements of Practice 08/1991 and 01/2006

3.   The meaning of "discover"

3.1   Introduction

The fundamental ingredient of a discovery assessment is that HMRC have "discovered" an under-assessment. This hurdle has long existed, pre-dating the self-assessment rules by many years. Indeed, the principal definition of what is necessary to substantiate a discovery went back more than 100 years. Although the statute was changed in 2022, the change did not affect the need for a relevant discovery to have been made; instead, it changed the definition of what amounted to a relevant discovery.

It should be noted that, despite a discovery being a fundamental pre-condition for a discovery assessment, many practitioners and HMRC officers have wrongly assumed that this hurdle was abolished (or somehow watered down) when self-assessment was introduced, leaving only the two conditions discussed in **Chapters 5 and 6**.

Indeed, it is common to hear it suggested that satisfaction of either of those two conditions should be referred to as the requisite discovery. That approach is wrong.

3.2   Who must make the discovery?

3.2.1   Need for an officer

It is clear from s. 29(1) itself that a discovery must be made by an HMRC officer. Legislation since introduced in 2020 to address the problem of automated penalties has now declared that "[a]nything capable of being done by an officer … may be done by HMRC (whether by means involving the use of a computer or otherwise)". The scope and precise meaning of this provision remains unclear and has already been the subject of conflicting tribunal decisions. However, for the time being, it is assumed that there must be some human thought process involved in the making of a discovery, the human in question being an HMRC officer (or Commissioner).

Indeed, in *Marano*, HMRC accepted that HMRC functions must, ultimately, be carried out by human agency (such humans being HMRC officers) and not in a wholly automated fashion. Despite that, the Upper Tribunal proceeded to say that any decision bearing HMRC's logo must be assumed to have been validly made unless the contrary can be proven.

Law: TMA 1970, s. 29(1); FA 2020, s. 103

Case: *Marano v HMRC* [2023] UKUT 113 (TCC)

3.2.2 Cases where multiple officers involved

Even prior to FA 2020, when an investigation was carried out by a team of officers, the question arose as to which member(s) of that team might make the discovery.

In *Carter*, HMRC sought to rely on statements in *Tutty* and *Gray* to support the proposition that any discovery "must be [by] an officer who has examined the [relevant] return". The FTT, however, disagreed. It held:

> "Whilst I accept that a discovery is only made where an officer, who is in possession of both the facts relating to the particular taxpayer and a knowledge of the relevant tax law, becomes aware of the loss of tax, that conclusion does not require the officer to be in possession of the relevant information as a result of examining the physical return. An officer might equally reach that level of awareness from information, which is extracted from a return, but held in some other form (physical or electronic), or from information provided to him or her by a colleague."

Indeed, in the author's view, the earlier decisions did not even support the proposition argued for by HMRC.

It should be noted that this question arose in the context of a challenge to a discovery assessment on the grounds of staleness. Following the Supreme Court's decision in *Tooth*, however, this is likely now to be of only academic interest.

Cases: *Tutty v HMRC* [2019] UKFTT 3 (TC); *Gray v HMRC* [2019] UKFTT 213 (TC); *Carter & Kennedy v HMRC* [2020] UKFTT 179 (TC); *HMRC v Tooth* [2021] UKSC 17

3.2.3 Identifying the officer(s) involved

It is not necessary for the officer who makes the discovery to be identifiable from any notice of the assessment (see **9.1.1**).

3.3   What is a discovery?

3.3.1   What must be discovered?

This basic question can often be answered wrongly. For example, it is very common to see HMRC quoting from (or, worse, paraphrasing) the Upper Tribunal's decision in *Charlton* as follows:

> "All that is required is that it has newly appeared to an officer, acting honestly and reasonably, that there is an insufficiency in an assessment. That can be for any reason, including a change of view, change of opinion, or correction of an oversight."

For the avoidance of doubt, the author has no issues with what the Upper Tribunal said in that passage. However, context is everything. The point is that s. 29(1) is very specific as to what must be discovered for the purposes of a discovery assessment.

Following amendments enacted in FA 2022, a discovery must be one or more of the following:

- that an amount of income tax or CGT ought to have been assessed but has not been assessed;
- that an assessment to tax is or has become insufficient; or
- that any relief that has been given is or has become excessive.

For the pre-FA 2022 position, see **3.8**.

The retroactive nature of the FA 2022 changes means that, in most cases, it will be the current (newer) version of s. 29 that should be examined by the courts and tribunals, irrespective of when the relevant assessment was made. See **3.8.5**.

These three situations are often abbreviated as "a loss of tax", which broadly (although not exactly) covers the statutory test.

As made clear by the Court of Appeal in *Tooth*, the important point is that what is claimed to have been discovered must fall within at least one of those three descriptions. Otherwise, the purported discovery is simply irrelevant for the purposes of any assessment.

Example

Benjamin's 2022 tax return was submitted late on 15 March 2023. An HMRC officer discovers this fact on 10 November 2023.

Whilst learning that the tax return was late might well be a discovery in the general sense of the word, it is not a relevant discovery for the purposes of s. 29(1).

In short, HMRC need to discover that there is a perceived loss of tax.

Law: TMA 1970, s. 29(1)

Cases: *HMRC v Charlton (and others)* [2012] UKUT 770 (TCC); *HMRC v Tooth* [2019] EWCA Civ 826

Connection between the discovery and the assessment

The *Wilkes* case confirmed that the subject matter of any discovery assessment must relate to the underlying discovery. In other words, the assessment must do no more than remedy the loss of tax discovered.

Thus, to take an extreme example, a discovery that interest has been under-assessed is in itself insufficient to justify any assessment that seeks to bring chargeable gains newly into charge.

Case: *HMRC v Wilkes* [2022] EWCA Civ 1612

"Tax that ought to have been assessed"

As discussed at **3.8**, the FA 2022 amendment to the wording of s. 29(1)(a) addresses the situation highlighted in *Wilkes* where a taxpayer had a latent tax liability but had not been required by HMRC to submit a tax return. *Wilkes* was a case involving unpaid high income child benefit charge (HICBC), but the case confirmed the existence of an anomaly that can arise in the case of other standalone tax charges (such as unauthorised payment charges imposed under the pensions rules).

However, the revised wording could potentially give rise to another legal argument with a view to demonstrating that what is discovered falls outside the scope of the three situations identified in s. 29(1).

As can be seen at **3.3.1**, the new version of s. 29(1)(a) turns on a discovery that tax that ought to have been assessed has not been assessed. The question that arises is whether this can be satisfied in a case where the taxpayer has not been required to submit a tax return. In the absence of such a requirement, the taxpayer might still argue that there was no amount of tax that "*ought* to have been assessed", such an obligation arising only once a notice to file a return is given.

In *Wilkes*, the Court of Appeal appeared to accept that a taxpayer's duty to notify chargeability (which should then lead to a notice to file being issued) should be sufficient to satisfy this statutory hurdle.

However, this then requires close analysis of whether the taxpayer was in fact due to notify chargeability under s. 7. That was originally drafted so as to excuse taxpayers whose income was subject to tax at source (mainly PAYE taxpayers). However, it was amended to require notification of chargeability in cases where the HICBC was payable. Accordingly, the revised wording of s. 29(1)(a) is likely to catch individuals who are liable for the HICBC but who fail to notify HMRC.

On the other hand, there were other standalone tax charges that did not give rise to any similar notification obligation, meaning that it remains arguable that (even with the revised wording of s. 29(1)(a)) there is not an amount of tax that "ought" to have been assessed. However, this potential anomaly was also removed by FA 2022, albeit only in respect of 2021-22 and later tax years. Now, all standalone charges (and not just HICBC) must give rise to a notification duty. Accordingly, the argument remains viable in respect of earlier years.

Law: TMA 1970, s. 7, 8, 29(1)(a); FA 2022, s. 98
Case: *HMRC v Wilkes* [2022] EWCA Civ 1612

3.3.2   *The moment of discovery – crossing a threshold*

Inherent in the word "discover" itself is the fact that there must be a change of position in the mind of the HMRC officer. As the Upper Tribunal put it in *Charlton*:

> "... the word 'discovers' does connote change, in the sense of a threshold being crossed. At one point an officer is not of the view that there is an insufficiency such that an assessment ought to be raised, and at another he is of that view."

The Supreme Court implicitly endorsed this definition of discovery in *Tooth*.

Cases: *HMRC v Charlton (and others)* [2012] UKUT 770 (TCC); *HMRC v Tooth* [2021] UKSC 17

3.3.3 Facts and laws may be discovered

Under English law, there has traditionally been a distinction between fact and law. Although the distinction has been somewhat eroded, it is still evident in the restrictions on matters that may be the subject of appeal from the FTT to the Upper Tribunal.

With this distinction in mind, it was once argued up to the House of Lords that a discovery had to be of a fact and that learning the true meaning of a law could not form the basis of a discovery assessment. The underlying logic is that people in general (and tax officers in particular) are sometimes thought to be deemed to know the law. However, in *Cenlon*, the House of Lords emphasised that learning the true meaning of a law was as much a discovery as finding out a particular fact.

As Viscount Simonds held (with emphasis added):

> "I can see no reason for saying that a discovery of undercharge can only arise where a new fact has been discovered. The words are apt to include *any* case in which for any reason it newly appears that the taxpayer has been undercharged and the context supports rather than detracts from this interpretation."

As for the argument that everyone is supposed to know the law, Lord Denning set out the correct position:

> "Mr Shelbourne said that 'discovery' means finding out something new about the facts. It does not mean a change of mind about the law. He said that everyone is presumed to know the law, even an inspector of taxes. I am afraid I cannot agree with Mr Shelbourne about this. It is a mistake to say that everyone is presumed to know the law. The true proposition is that no one is to be excused from doing his duty by pleading that he did not know the law. Every lawyer who, in his researches in the books, finds out that he was mistaken about the law, makes a discovery. So also does an inspector of taxes."

For completeness, it should also be noted that Lord Denning's "true proposition" does not preclude taxpayers from claiming reasonable excuse for not knowing their taxing and reporting obligations. That topic, however, is outside the scope of this text.

Case: *Cenlon Finance Co Ltd v Ellwood* (1962) 40 TC 176

Something "new"

The above extract from the speech of Viscount Simonds refers to the essential concept of a discovery being something that "newly appears". With this in mind, it was made clear in *Beagles* that it is not possible to make the same discovery twice:

> "Whilst we accept that it might be possible for an officer to discover the same insufficiency in a return more than once if it is for different reasons, it is not, in our view, possible for an officer to make the same discovery twice for the same reasons. The insufficiency cannot 'newly appear' to the officer for a second time."

This can still create some misunderstanding. The author's view (reinforced by the context of the *Beagles* case) is that a belief that a particular set of arrangements does not give the tax saving hoped for represents a discovery for these purposes. Accordingly, if a further reason for holding that same view emerges at a later date, then that does not represent a separate discovery: the original reason (that the arrangements are not tax-effective) remains unchanged (even if the underlying basis for that conclusion has changed).

Nevertheless, once again, the Supreme Court's decision in *Tooth* makes this point of limited relevance. As the court concluded:

> "[the wording] 'it newly appears ...' was a reference to the state of mind of the person said to have made the discovery, to whom it 'newly appears' that an assessment to tax is insufficient. A discovery is a particular event in time, and does not cease to be such with the passage of time."

Cases: *Beagles v HMRC* [2018] UKUT 380 (TCC); *HMRC v Tooth* [2021] UKSC 17

3.3.4   What level of knowledge constitutes a discovery?

The English word "discover" is suggestive of an individual becoming aware of something. However, in life and tax in particular, matters are usually far from black and white.

Indeed, a "fact" cannot be determined with any sense of legal certainty until it constitutes a final finding of a court. Similarly, the correct interpretation of any legal proposition cannot be finally confirmed until it is the subject of a ruling of the Supreme Court (which can, in any event, change its mind in later cases).

If one were to apply this meaning of "discovery", it would be virtually impossible for an HMRC officer to discover anything, as the discovery must inevitably precede the legal process under which the subject matter of the alleged discovery will be tested. Consequently, a different meaning is applied in the tax context.

The leading case is that of *Aramayo*. There the various judges defined "discovers" as follows:

> "... it would seem therefore most unlikely that the legislation should have intended by the word discover that he was to ascertain by legal evidence. It provides for a later trial, if I may call it so, the question when either party appeals. This is not the time for legal evidence, and it seems to me to be quite clear that the word 'discover' cannot mean ascertain by legal evidence; it means, in my opinion, simply 'comes to the conclusion' from the examination he makes, and, if he likes, from any information he receives." (per Bray J)

> "I think that word means 'has reason to believe'." (per Avory J)

> "Now if you take the word 'discovers', as I think it clearly was intended to be taken, as merely an alternative to 'find' or 'satisfy himself', the difficulty disappears." (per Lush J)

This is an extremely wide definition (although not unreasonably so).

It should be noted that the subsequent case of *Hooper* added a small restriction to the definition: that is simply that the officer reaching the conclusion must be acting reasonably and honestly. In other words, the conclusion reached must be a reasonable one from the evidence before the officer.

In short, a discovery requires more than mere speculation. It cannot be based on a mere whim.

The key ingredients were summarised by the Upper Tribunal in *Anderson*. In particular:

"the concept of an officer discovering something involves, in the first place, an actual officer having a particular state of mind in relation to the relevant matter; this involves the application of a subjective test;

the concept of an officer discovering something involves, in the second place, the officer's state of mind satisfying some objective criterion; this involves the application of an objective test;

if the officer's state of mind does not satisfy the relevant subjective test and the relevant objective test, then the officer's state of mind is insufficient for there to be a discovery for the purposes of subsection (1);

s 29(1) also refers to the opinion of the officer as to what ought to be charged to make good the loss of tax; accordingly, the officer has to form a relevant opinion and such an opinion has to satisfy some objective criterion."

In *Daisley*, the tribunal concluded that the test of reasonableness should be applied at the time of the alleged discovery and not (if significantly later) at the time the consequential assessment is made. That case was decided before the Supreme Court's decision in *Tooth* and the point might therefore be academic now. Alternatively, one possible consequence of the *Tooth* decision is that an officer making a reasonable discovery on day 1 may not actually be permitted to make the assessment if, in the meantime, there is no longer any reasonable belief in the under-assessment.

Indeed, in *Kamran*, a case which also preceded *Tooth*, the tribunal noted that once a discovery is made (which requires the officer's reasonable view), the amount of the assessment must continue to be reasonable and not be "capricious or arbitrary".

Cases: *R v Kensington Income Tax Commissioners (ex parte Aramayo)* (1913) 6 TC 279; *R v Commissioners of Taxes for St Giles and St George Bloomsbury (ex parte Hooper)* (1915) 7 TC 59; *Anderson v HMRC* [2018] UKUT 159 (TCC); *Daisley v National Crime Agency* [2018] UKFTT 708 (TC); *Kamran v HMRC* [2019] UKFTT 257 (TC); *HMRC v Tooth* [2021] UKSC 17

Theoretical difficulties with the meaning of "discover"

In *Corbally-Stourton*, the Special Commissioner described the test as follows:

> "It seems to me clear that both these judges and the legislation do not require the inspector to be certain beyond all doubt that there is an insufficiency; what is required is that he comes to the conclusion on the information available to him and the law as he understands it, that it is more likely than not that there is an insufficiency. I shall call this a conclusion that it is probable that there is an insufficiency."

This effectively suggested a "more than 50% likelihood".

Although largely adopting the approach set out by the Special Commissioner elsewhere in his decision, the Court of Appeal in *Lansdowne* took issue with this "more likely than not" approach to HMRC's powers of discovery. Strictly speaking, the comments in *Lansdowne* were directed at the Special Commissioner's use of the test in the context of s. 29(5). Nevertheless, it is considered that the objection is just as apt (if not more so) in the context of s. 29(1) itself. As Moses LJ said:

> "I think there is a danger in substituting wording appropriate to standards of proof for the statutory condition."

The difficulty (perhaps inherent in Moses LJ's judgment) is that none of the case law to date actually defines with complete accuracy the circumstances in which HMRC can be said to have made a discovery (or, in the alternative, it is possible that HMRC are frequently making assessments in cases where they have not actually made a proper discovery).

For example, suppose one has a situation in which a statutory provision has two equally possible interpretations. Alternatively, suppose one has a case in which two witnesses (perhaps former spouses) are giving conflicting evidence – it is certain that one is right and that one is wrong, but impossible to determine which. In both cases, assume that the different conclusions will lead to different tax outcomes. These are truly 50-50 decisions and no HMRC officer, acting honestly and reasonably, could believe that one outcome is any more likely than the other.

Accordingly, no officer would be able to say that he or she "has reason to believe" that tax has been underpaid or that he or she can "satisfy himself [or herself]" or "conclude" that there has been an earlier under-assessment. Nevertheless, it would seem unreasonable to deny the officer the right to make an assessment so as to allow the matter to be adjudicated on in the tribunal.

Accordingly, most of the current case law suggests that a discovery assessment would not be strictly permissible in such 50-50 cases. In practice, however, it is likely that the officer will be able to justify making an assessment (or will simply assert a justification) and, therefore, this theoretical problem is unlikely to manifest itself.

However, in *Anderson*, the Upper Tribunal summarised the test and commented on it as follows:

> "The officer must believe that the information available to him points in the direction of there being an insufficiency of tax.
>
> That formulation, in our judgment, acknowledges both that the discovery must be something more than suspicion of an insufficiency of tax and that it need not go so far as a conclusion that an insufficiency of tax is more probable than not."

As later confirmed by the Court of Appeal in *Clark*, the test as to what constitutes a discovery "must be a practical and workable test".

Cases: *Corbally-Stourton v HMRC* (2008) Sp C 692; *HMRC v Lansdowne Partners LP* [2011] EWCA Civ 1578; *Anderson v HMRC* [2018] UKUT 159 (TCC); *Clark v HMRC* [2020] EWCA Civ 204

3.3.5   Situations that might constitute a discovery

A discovery can arise in very many different situations – effectively any case in which HMRC might seek to investigate a taxpayer's affairs.

These can include:

- conducting a routine investigation (perhaps covering several tax years) in which one or more notices of enquiry were not issued in time;
- an HMRC investigation into one taxpayer identifying another taxpayer who is likely to have participated in similar arrangements (for example, fellow directors or co-participants in a tax avoidance scheme);

- HMRC's intelligence-gathering identifying possible sources of undisclosed income (through newspaper/internet articles or advertisements or even old-fashioned walking around a neighbourhood (such as identifying pop-up car parking arrangements in the Wimbledon area during the tennis tournament)); and

- HMRC acting on third-party tip-offs (for example, former spouses, overseas tax authorities or stolen data from commercial organisations). Alternatively, the taxpayer might be the source of the original lead.

3.3.6 *"Protective assessments"*

It is common for HMRC to make what they call "protective assessments", especially if a time limit (see **Chapter 8**) is about to expire.

As was finally recognised in *Ritchie*, the concept of a "protective assessment" is not recognised by the statute and, as a result, many such assessments may well be invalid. As is always the case, the key is the underlying facts rather than the terminology used by HMRC:

- If HMRC are in the course of an investigation, but they already have reason to believe that tax has been underpaid for the year in question, then they can justifiably make an assessment ahead of an impending time limit so as to protect their position, pending the culmination of the ongoing investigation. Indeed, not to do so would be a dereliction of an officer's duty.

- However, where an officer has no reason to believe that tax has been underpaid (but there is merely the suspicion of an underpayment), a protective assessment may be challenged on the ground that there is no underlying discovery. It should be noted, however, that a reason to suspect an underpayment can be sufficient to justify an information notice under Schedule 36 (see **Chapter 11**).

Furthermore, as the Court of Appeal made clear in *Clark*, if the case proceeds on appeal, a tribunal must then focus on the discovery allegedly made at the time of the assessment, rather than on what might subsequently be discovered. However, when determining what comprises that earlier discovery, it is necessary to take a broad approach. Therefore, if an officer focuses on one particular event as crystallising the tax liability, it can still be appropriate to consider related events (at least in a situation where the evidence of the original discovery is stated in provisional terms).

Law: FA 2008, Sch. 36, para. 21(6)

Cases: *Ritchie & Ritchie v HMRC* [2017] UKFTT 449 (TC); *Clark v HMRC* [2020] EWCA Civ 204

3.3.7   Supporting an asserted discovery

In many such cases, the information available to HMRC will be quite limited and officers will be required to undertake some considerable guesswork to demonstrate that a discovery has been made. However, within certain bounds, the case law supports such methods, as long as they are conducted reasonably.

The *Islam* case demonstrates what can happen if unreasonable methods are adopted. The case concerned an investigation into a restaurant where the tribunal noted a number of concerns with the taxpayer's case. However, those concerns were ultimately irrelevant because HMRC's own approach in conducting the investigation, and the evidence put forward to substantiate the alleged discovery, gave rise to what the tribunal called "huge difficulties". As the tribunal was "simply not persuaded that HMRC have discharged the burden of proof", it had no alternative but to allow the appeals.

Case: *Islam v HMRC* [2022] UKFTT 188 (TC)

Capital statements

For example, HMRC might encounter a taxpayer whose known income and capital sources seem insufficient to support the lifestyle which the taxpayer is leading. As held in the case of *Jonas v Bamford*:

> "There can be no doubt at all that the Inspector of Taxes discovered that Mr Jonas was the possessor of resources which would not be explained by reference to known sources of capital and income. This is virtually the classic case of 'discovery'. In law, indeed, very little is required to constitute a case of 'discovery': see *Cenlon Finance Co Ltd v Ellwood*."

Case: *Jonas v Bamford (HM Inspector of Taxes)* (1973) 51 TC 1

Presumption of continuity

Another tool available to HMRC is the presumption of continuity: if a mistake is known (perhaps through a self-assessment enquiry) to have been made (perhaps due to ignorance of the law or due to an accounting deficiency), it might be reasonable to assume that a similar error has occurred in other years. Again, the leading authority is the case of *Jonas v Bamford* where the court held:

> "... so far as the discovery point is concerned, once the Inspector comes to the conclusion that, on the facts which he has discovered, Mr Jonas has additional income beyond that which he has so far declared to the Inspector, then the usual presumption of continuity will apply. The situation will be presumed to go on until there is some change in the situation, the onus of proof of which is clearly on the taxpayer."

Bekoe gives the following guidance:

> "... any such assumption must depend on an established pattern of behaviour or circumstances which may be assumed to continue because they form a predictable pattern."

The author is attracted by the proposition that the presumption of continuity can apply in either direction: knowledge of a particular state of affairs in year 2 should mean that, all things being equal, an officer is entitled to assume a similar state of affairs both in years 1 and 3 (and beyond, of course).

However, some decisions of the FTT – which are not binding precedents – have cast doubt on this, suggesting instead that an officer may go only forwards in time.

For example, in *Chapman*, the tribunal considered the above extract from *Jonas v Bamford* but continued (with emphasis in the original):

> "The presumption *goes on until there is some change*. The presumption as expressed in that case looks to the future and not the past. It is difficult to see how one can apply such a presumption based on the Enquiry Year to the earlier years."

The later case of *Gui Hui Dong* rejected such contentions although it is not clear whether it had been specifically referred to *Chapman*.

Although the point was not raised in *Stirling*, that was a case in the Upper Tribunal that proceeded on the basis that the presumption can work in both directions.

Another case (*Syed*) initially appears to reject the presumption as a tool altogether. However, a close reading suggests that it is saying no more (as with all such tools) than that it should be applied with care. In particular, as with any presumption, it is capable of rebuttal.

A change of circumstances can be sufficient to counter the presumption and therefore, in some cases, will defeat the asserted discovery. Although the author does not agree with the end result, the *Kamran* case illustrates how the presumption of continuity can be rebutted.

Kamran was a case involving a landlord with a tenant who had made a housing benefit claim. HMRC argued that the presumption of continuity justified a "discovery" in respect of other tax years. However, the tribunal disagreed, pointing out that a tenant's housing benefit claim is something that would not run from year to year, but would need to be renewed if applicable. The author doubts that the tribunal was right to be so cautious in this regard, as the evidence of housing benefit by a supposed tenant would have been a reason to presume that the property was being let out to that or another tenant from year to year. Accordingly, in that case, it seems that the presumption should have been available to HMRC, although of course potentially capable of rebuttal by some other means.

Other examples of a presumption being rebutted are as follows:

- In *Gaughan*, the enquiry year showed the understatement of turnover because of missing certificates under the Construction Industry Scheme. However, in the earlier years subject to discovery assessments, the records in that regard at least were complete. Therefore, it was not appropriate to roll back the adjusted profits from the enquiry year.

- Similarly, in *Chapman*, the tribunal was quite critical of HMRC's re-creation of one year's accounts and the backdating of them to earlier years, when it was quite clear that the underlying facts were different in those other years.

- In *Cardazzone*, explicable one-off errors in one tax year could not be relied upon by HMRC under the presumption of continuity to constitute a discovery in relation to another year.

- In *Stirling*, the tribunal noted the qualitative and quantitative changes in the business which allowed the presumption to be rebutted for most years under enquiry. Furthermore, the tribunal noted that the pressure on the bookkeeper which led to the identified errors was relevant in only a relatively short period.

- In *Amini*, the tribunal considered that the presumption had been rebutted in a case where the officer had overlooked the taxpayer's childcare responsibilities in some years which reduced her ability to carry out paid work for more than 15 hours a week.

Cases: *Jonas v Bamford (HM Inspector of Taxes)* (1973) 51 TC 1; *Bekoe v HMRC* [2017] UKFTT 772 (TC); *Gaughan v HMRC* (2006) Sp C 575; *Syed v HMRC* [2011] UKFTT 315 (TC); *Chapman v HMRC* [2011] UKFTT 756 (TC); *Gui Hui Dong v National Crime Agency* [2014] UKFTT 128 (TC); *Cardazzone v HMRC* [2014] UKFTT 357 (TC); *Kamran v HMRC* [2019] UKFTT 257 (TC); *Stirling Jewellers (Dudley) Ltd v HMRC* [2020] UKUT 245 (TCC); *Amini v HMRC* [2021] UKFTT 289 (TC)

Business economics exercises

Another method traditionally employed by HMRC investigators involves comparing a business's declared takings and expenses with what HMRC might consider to be industry norms. Whilst these exercises might well identify areas of risk, worthy of further investigation, they should very rarely (if ever) form the basis of an asserted discovery. As the Special Commissioner concluded in *Farthings Steak House*:

> "The Inland Revenue have failed to find any unaccounted for bankings or unaccounted for expenditure or any unaccounted for capital accretions. Their efforts have thus been devoted to the preparation of several business economic exercises, several of which have been shown to be inaccurate or just plain wrong. In any event in my judgment business economic exercises alone can rarely if ever justify the sort of attack mounted by the Inland Revenue in these appeals."

Indeed, *Farthings Steak House* was the first case in which the then Inland Revenue were obliged to pay a taxpayer the costs of a hearing before the Special Commissioners on the basis of "wholly unreasonable conduct" – the particularly onerous test that was then in force.

Case: *Scott & Anor (t/a Farthings Steak House) v McDonald (HM Inspector of Taxes)* (1996) Sp C 91

Actions of other taxpayers

In *Anderson*, a discovery was held to be valid on the basis that HMRC had formed a view about the ineffectiveness of arrangements entered by other participants of a tax avoidance scheme. This seems uncontroversial. However, the tribunal went further to suggest that an officer could attribute one taxpayer's lack of time spent in the business (sufficient hours being a necessary ingredient for the loss relief claimed being available) to another. The author respectfully disagrees with that view as there should be a factual basis for considering that the specific taxpayer in question is not entitled to the relief claimed.

Case: *Anderson v HMRC* [2018] UKUT 159 (TCC)

Mismatch of information

In *Wilby*, a case concerning SDLT, the FTT considered that a mismatch between the purchase price shown on the Land Registry and that on the SDLT return was a sufficient basis to justify a discovery assessment.

Case: *Wilby v HMRC* [2022] UKFTT 348 (TC)

3.4 Making rediscoveries

3.4.1 Assessing on the basis of old information

As noted at **3.3.3**, in addition to the idea of crossing a threshold, the word "discover" also implies the need for something new: the additional detail that takes an officer from one side of the threshold to the other.

This focus on the new detail led to the question as to whether a discovery assessment could be invalid if the newness of that detail had turned stale. Although the concept of staleness has since been largely defeated by the Supreme Court in *Tooth*, the Supreme Court did support the idea that irrational delays might still be capable of challenge. This is discussed more fully at **3.9.6**.

Case: *HMRC v Tooth* [2021] UKSC 17

3.4.2 HMRC revisiting prior decisions

There will be cases where an officer has plainly overlooked a matter previously provided to him or her. As noted above, this will not usually preclude a discovery taking place later once the officer realises his or her error.

However, in cases where there has been a prior agreement between the taxpayer and HMRC which leads to a negotiated settlement under TMA 1970, s. 54, the statute provides that that agreement precludes HMRC from pursuing the matter further by making a fresh discovery assessment. This applies, however, only where there was material before the original officer which could have or should have been taken into account when the original agreement was reached. The leading case is *Olin* where the House of Lords concluded:

> "The situation must be viewed objectively, from the point of view of whether the inspector's agreement to the relevant computation, having regard to the surrounding circumstances including all the material known to be in his possession, was such as to lead a reasonable man to the conclusion that he had decided to admit the claim which had been made."

HMRC have responded to *Olin* in their published guidance and will consider themselves able to make a discovery in cases where:

- a particular point underlying an agreement was not fundamental to the agreement;
- there has been fraudulent or negligent conduct leading to an under-assessment;
- there has been the misleading or misinforming of an officer about the particular matter at issue;
- the agreement was subject to an arithmetical error which had not been spotted when the agreement was reached; or
- the error was clearly unintended.

The relevance of *Olin* is somewhat limited in the self-assessment era because fewer agreements are now reached under the terms of s. 54. Nevertheless, once an appealable decision has been issued, any resolution which does not involve the tribunal comes within s. 54 (or is deemed to) and is therefore treated as having been decided by the tribunal.

Nevertheless, in *Easinghall*, the Upper Tribunal did conclude that a successful appeal against a discovery assessment had the effect of precluding HMRC from raising the same point in a statutory enquiry that was subsequently opened into the taxpayer's return. The author is not convinced about the correctness of the *Easinghall* decision. Nevertheless, it is a decision binding on the FTT.

It should also be noted that the *Easinghall* decision is consistent with HMRC guidance at SP 8/91 where they say that they will respect a taxpayer's right to finality even if an earlier agreement has been reached otherwise than after the issue of an assessment. See also **Appendix 1**.

A related issue arose in the case of *Kelly*. HMRC had issued a discovery assessment in 2016 which they later withdrew on the basis that they considered it to be procedurally invalid. However, this withdrawal took place after the taxpayer's appeal had been notified to the tribunal. Given HMRC's decision to withdraw the assessment, the tribunal formally allowed Mr Kelly's appeal. HMRC then issued replacement assessments in 2017.

The tribunal queried the validity of the 2017 assessments, given that they seemed to replace ones previously withdrawn. In response, HMRC agreed that the 2017 assessments were indeed invalid, but then sought to argue that the 2016 assessments were both valid (notwithstanding HMRC's earlier stance) and still live (but subject to the amendments reflected in the 2017 assessments).

The tribunal considered that the unilateral decision of HMRC to withdraw the 2016 assessments did not amount to a s. 54 agreement and, therefore, would remain live until such time as any appeal was disposed of by the tribunal. However, the tribunal continued its analysis by referring to the formal notice given by the tribunal which allowed Mr Kelly's appeal against the 2016 assessments. Accordingly, HMRC were unable to resurrect them at a later date.

Law: TMA 1970, s. 54

Cases: *Scorer (HM Inspector of Taxes) v Olin Energy Systems Ltd* (1985) 58 TC 592; *Easinghall Ltd v HMRC* [2016] UKUT 105 (TCC); *Kelly v HMRC* [2021] UKFTT 162 (TC)

Guidance: *Statement of Practice* 08/1991

3.5 Timing of a discovery

3.5.1 Overview

In addition to any public law requirement that a discovery assessment must follow within a reasonable period after the underlying discovery (as discussed more fully at **3.9.6**), there are also statutory time limits which prevent HMRC from making discovery assessments after particular dates (see **Chapter 8** below).

However, what is not expressly covered by the legislation is whether there are restrictions on when the underlying discovery itself can take place.

Of course, the discovery must precede the assessment. But can a discovery ever be too early? The case law gave two conflicting views, which were resolved only in 2023.

3.5.2 The alternative views

Given the importance of the enquiry mechanism, there is a strong argument to suggest that the discovery "threshold" must not be crossed during the enquiry window or in the course of a live enquiry. In other words, should an HMRC officer discover something whilst still being permitted to deal with the matter in the course of an enquiry, then that is precisely what the officer should do.

Indeed, one of the conditions for a discovery assessment (see **Chapter 6** below) concerns the quality of information available to HMRC at the end of the enquiry window (or, in the case where an actual enquiry has been opened, when the enquiry closes). Consequently, the discovery provisions cannot be properly considered until after the enquiry window closes.

This was precisely the approach taken by the Special Commissioner in *Lee* when he said (albeit in a slightly different context):

"One limit is that the section 29 powers can only be used after either the 'window' under section 9A has passed in respect of that tax return or the Officer has closed an enquiry into that tax return: section 29(5)."

On the other hand, it should be remembered that discovery assessments can be made in cases where there has not actually been any return and, therefore, the concept of the enquiry window is of no relevance. Furthermore, there is no express provision in the legislation which requires the discovery to be made at any particular time. In light of this, the FTT in *Taube* expressed the following alternative view:

"In our view the statutory rules permit a discovery either before or after the time for opening an enquiry has expired, the only timing constraint being the time limit for the making of the assessment in section 34."

HMRC's own guidance made clear that they favoured the latter approach. It read:

"There may be occasions when an open enquiry window for the post-enquiry year exists, but it is easier and quicker to make a discovery assessment or recognise the ability to do so, in the terms of a contract settlement."

The matter was the subject of full discussion in *Norton*. Overturning the FTT on the point, the Upper Tribunal concluded that any question as to an assessment's procedural validity should be focused on the validity at the time the assessment is made. That approach means that s. 29(5) must be assumed to be looking *back* at the end of any enquiry window. Accordingly, the tribunal concluded that a discovery assessment may not be made if the enquiry window is still open.

On the other hand, the Upper Tribunal did not go so far as to suggest that *Taube* was wrong either. What *Norton* says is that a discovery assessment (at least one relying on s. 29(5)) cannot be made during the enquiry window. However, no comment was made on what happened in *Taube* where the discovery was made during the enquiry window but the assessment itself was made after the window had closed.

Furthermore, the *Norton* case concerned only discovery assessments relying on s. 29(5) and not those relying on s. 29(4). HMRC's updated manual makes it clear that HMRC's view has been revised only in relation to s. 29(5):

> "Legally an officer can make a discovery assessment whilst the enquiry window is open so long as the loss of tax was caused carelessly or deliberately."

It is true that some of the reasoning in *Norton* cannot be applied to s. 29(4) cases. However, the combination of the primacy of the enquiry procedure and the fact that s. 29(4) and s. 29(5) both follow on from s. 29(3) suggests that there remains a good argument that no discovery assessment may be made during the enquiry window. HMRC accordingly advise their officers:

> "In practice a discovery assessment should not normally be made where ... a SA return has been received and the enquiry window is open – instead open an enquiry[.]"

Law: TMA 1970, s. 9A, 29, 34

Cases: *Lee v HMRC* (2008) Sp C 715; *Trustees of the Bessie Taube Discretionary Settlement Trust v HMRC (and others)* [2010] UKFTT 473 (TC); *Norton v HMRC* [2023] UKUT 48 (TCC)

Guidance: EM 2040, 3265

3.6   Other taxes

3.6.1   Corporation tax

The equivalent provisions

The equivalent power is found in FA 1998, Sch. 18, para. 41(1).

Discovery determinations

In addition, an HMRC officer can make discovery determinations in cases where:

- the officer makes a discovery; and
- that discovery is that a company tax return incorrectly states either:
    - an amount that affects (or may affect) the tax payable by that company for another period; or

    o an amount that affects (or may affect) the tax liability of another company.

Discovery determinations are subject to the same rules as discovery assessments.

Law: FA 1998, Sch. 18, para. 41(2)

Excessive group relief

A further corporation tax power is available to HMRC in cases where a discovery is made that a company has obtained excessive group relief. Assessments may be made in such circumstances independently of any power to make a discovery assessment under para. 41.

Law: FA 1998, Sch. 18, para. 76

Surplus dual inclusion income

A further corporation tax power is available to HMRC in the context of the hybrid and other mismatches regime.

In cases where there has been an excessive allocation claim for surplus dual inclusion income. Assessments may be made in such circumstances independently of any power to make a discovery assessment under para. 41.

Law: FA 1998, Sch. 18, para. 77K

Excessive terminal film loss relief

There is a further corporation tax power available to HMRC in cases where a discovery is made that a company has obtained excessive terminal loss relief on films. Assessments may be made in such circumstances independently of any power to make a discovery assessment under para. 41.

Law: SI 2007/678, reg. 15

3.6.2   SDLT

The equivalent provisions

The equivalent power to make a discovery assessment is found in FA 2003, Sch. 10, para. 28. As noted in *Tutty*, there was no practical difference arising from the fact that para. 28 refers to "the Inland Revenue".

Unlike s. 29, which refers to a tax year, para. 28 refers to a chargeable transaction. In *Field*, that was potentially significant because there were two transactions in question: the actual land transaction and a notional one deemed to take place under the anti-avoidance provisions in FA 2003, s. 75A. However, the tribunal held that the reference to chargeable transaction in para. 28 "is wide enough to allow HMRC to look at all the facts and circumstances surrounding that transaction, including the 'scheme transactions' and the notional land transaction".

Law: FA 2003, s. 75A

Cases: *Tutty v HMRC* [2019] UKFTT 3 (TC); *G C Field & Sons Ltd v HMRC* [2021] UKFTT 297 (TC)

3.6.3   ATED

The equivalent provisions

The equivalent power to make a discovery assessment is found in FA 2013, Sch. 33, para. 21.

3.7   Other discovery provisions

3.7.1   Non-resident CGT (for disposals before 6 April 2019)

The equivalent provisions

The equivalent provisions to make a discovery assessment are found in TMA 1970, s. 29A(1), (2). When a discovery is made, HMRC may determine (rather than assess) the additional tax due.

Law: TMA 1970, former s. 29A(1), (2)

3.7.2   Partnership returns

The equivalent provisions

The equivalent provisions are found in TMA 1970, s. 30B(1). When a discovery is made HMRC may amend the partnership return to repair any error discovered.

In such cases, the officer may also amend each partner's return to give effect to any changes made to the partnership return.

However, as confirmed in *Odey*, s. 30B is applicable only in cases where there is a shortfall in declared partnership profits: it cannot be used to reallocate declared profits between different partners.

Law: TMA 1970, s. 30B(1), (2)

Case: *Odey Asset Management LLP v HMRC* [2021] UKFTT 31 (TC)

3.7.3   Digital services tax

The equivalent power in relation to the digital services tax is found in FA 2020, Sch. 8, para. 19.

Law: FA 2020, Sch. 8, para. 19(1)

3.7.4   Public interest business protection tax

The equivalent power in relation to the public interest business protection tax is found in FA 2022, Sch. 10, para. 18(1).

Law: FA 2022, Sch. 10, para. 18(1)

3.7.5   Multinational top-up tax

The equivalent power in relation to the multinational top-up tax is found in F(No. 2)A 2023, Sch. 14, para. 27.

Law: F(No. 2)A 2023, Sch. 14, para. 27

3.8   Discoveries and standalone tax charges

3.8.1   Introduction

The three categories of discovery that are often referred to using the simplified term "a loss of tax" are set out above at **3.3.1**. It was noted that the first of those categories was replaced by FA 2022.

Subject to a limited transitional provision (discussed at **3.8.6**), the amendment had retrospective effect in most cases. The change in the law was to correct a difficulty in relation to some standalone charges to tax that had become exposed in the case law.

3.8.2   Standalone charges

Although income tax is generally concerned with the aggregation of an individual's income from various sources and the application of specific tax rates to that income, there are certain situations where a person's tax liability is also subject to a standalone charge. For example:

- breaches of the pensions rules can lead to sanction charges; and
- family units in receipt of child benefit, where at least one member has income of more than £50,000, will see a recoupment of the family's child benefit by the imposition of what is known as the high income child benefit charge (HICBC).

In both of those cases, there is no additional "income" attributed to the individual liable for the charge; instead, that person's income tax liability (as otherwise calculated) is subject to an additional levy.

This gave rise to questions about the application of s. 29(1)(a) which, prior to FA 2022, was worded in terms of "income". That provision was engaged only if it was discovered:

> "that any income which ought to have been assessed to income tax, or chargeable gains which ought to have been assessed to capital gains tax, have not been assessed".

As discussed at **3.8.6**, this old version of s. 29(1)(a) will continue to apply for some cases.

3.8.3   The evolving case law

The point became particularly clear in two cases in 2018. In *Robertson*, the taxpayer was found to have become liable for the HICBC. Although that charge has the look of a provision that imposes tax on a portion of a taxpayer's income, the statute actually imposes a freestanding charge to income tax if certain conditions are met.

Accordingly, failure to self-assess for the charge would not amount to "income which ought to have been assessed to income tax ... hav[ing] not been assessed". As the taxpayer in that case had not self-assessed at all, the second limb of s. 29(1) was not satisfied and the third (concerning relief) was similarly irrelevant.

The same outcome was reached in *Monaghan* which concerned the pensions legislation and the provisions for unauthorised member payments. Again, the tribunal noted the nature of the statutory charge, which did not deem there to be income that should have been assessed. The tribunal also noted the specific modifications to the discovery rules conferred by the pensions legislation (also repealed by FA 2022) which did not extend to assessing the individual worker. The tribunal commented:

> "We can then only conclude that the legislation has either missed fire or it was a policy decision in 2004 or 2005 not to exercise a power to make an NSA [an assessment which is not a self-assessment, e.g. a discovery assessment] on an individual."

In both cases, the tribunal noted that a different outcome could have been reached had there been an inadequate self-assessment by the taxpayer (which would have engaged s. 29(1)(b)). The author is not entirely sure that this is in fact correct in relation to unauthorised payments, but this is not yet something that has been tested in the tribunal.

Although both *Robertson* and *Monaghan* were the subject of appeals by HMRC to the Upper Tribunal, the Upper Tribunal dealt with the *Robertson* appeal on a different basis and the *Monaghan* appeal was stayed for several years and appears no longer to be a live case.

However, in the meantime, the issue arose again in the context of three further HICBC cases in 2020: *Wilkes*, *Haslam* and *Wiseman*. *Wilkes* followed *Robertson* but, in *Haslam*, the FTT gave the legislation a "rectifying construction" saying that it was doing no more than correcting an obvious drafting anomaly. In *Wiseman*, however, the FTT considered that no rectifying construction was even necessary as the legislation (properly understood) permitted HICBC to be recovered by way of discovery assessments based on s. 29(1)(a).

HMRC chose to appeal against the one decision that they had lost (*Wilkes*) to the Upper Tribunal and subsequently to the Court of Appeal, which therefore had the benefit of considering the three different approaches by the three different compositions of the FTT. The Upper Tribunal and the Court of Appeal dismissed HMRC's appeals, finding that the (pre-2022) legislation precluded discovery assessments based on s. 29(1)(a) being used to recover HICBC and that the restrictive circumstances for a rectifying construction were not met.

It is understood that HMRC have accepted as final the decision of the Court of Appeal.

Law: TMA 1970, s. 29(1); ITEPA 2003, s. 681B; FA 2004, s. 208, 209, 255

Cases: *Monaghan v HMRC* [2018] UKFTT 156 (TC); *Robertson v HMRC* [2018] UKFTT 158 (TC); *Wilkes v HMRC* [2020] UKFTT 256 (TC); *Haslam v HMRC* [2020] UKFTT 304 (TC); *Wiseman v HMRC* [2020] UKFTT 383 (TC); *HMRC v Wilkes* [2021] UKUT 150 (TCC); *HMRC v Wilkes* [2022] EWCA Civ 1612

3.8.4   Statutory developments

Clearly concerned (and with justification) that the Court of Appeal would similarly find against HMRC, HMRC announced new legislation relatively soon after the Upper Tribunal's decision. Parliament has obliged and the law is now as reflected at **3.3.1**.

Whereas changes in assessing powers usually come into effect on or after the date on which the relevant Finance Act gets Royal Assent, the FA 2022 change was given retrospective effect, so as to enable the new wording to apply to an assessment (and, therefore, a discovery) that pre-dates the change being formally made. This is subject to a transitional provision that preserves the effect of the pre-2022 wording for certain cases that are already in the pipeline.

3.8.5   When does the new wording come into effect?

For any discovery assessment in relation to 2021-22 (or any later tax year), the new wording of s. 29(1)(a) applies without exception (irrespective of whether the assessment was made before or after Royal Assent was given to FA 2022).

Similarly, the old wording of s. 29(1)(a) as set out at **3.8.2** will continue to apply for most discovery assessments made in relation to 2020-21 and any earlier tax year. In other words, for most discovery assessments, there will be no retrospective change in the law.

However, so as to avoid further arguments similar to those in the *Wilkes* case, the new wording will generally be applied retrospectively to any discovery assessment that has been (or is) made in respect of the following matters:

- HICBC;
- recovery of surplus gift aid;

- short service refund lump sum and special lump sum death benefits charges, when it is the person to whom the amount is paid who is liable for the charge (as opposed to the scheme administrator); and

- unauthorised payments charges, unauthorised payments surcharges, lifetime allowance charges, annual allowance charges and overseas transfer charges.

However, even in those cases, the pre-2022 wording (which was the subject of the Court of Appeal's deliberations in the *Wilkes* case) will continue to apply in certain limited cases, as outlined in **3.8.6**.

Law: ITEPA 2003, Pt. 10, Ch. 8; FA 2004, s. 205, 206, 208, 209, 214, 227, 244A, Sch. 34; ITA 2007, s. 424; FA 2022, s. 97(3), (4)
Case: *HMRC v Wilkes* [2022] EWCA Civ 1612

3.8.6   Preservation of old wording for some cases

As noted at **3.8.5**, HMRC sought Parliament's help to avoid facing further arguments similar to those in the *Wilkes* case, even in respect of discovery assessments previously made. However, they were conscious that similar arguments were being lined up in other cases, which were awaiting the outcome of the *Wilkes* litigation before proceeding. HMRC realised that to deny them the opportunity to run the *Wilkes* argument would have been particularly unfair.

Accordingly, for any discovery assessments relating to 2020-21 or any earlier tax year (even if in respect of tax charges identified in the four bullet points set out at **3.8.5**), the pre-2022 wording will continue to apply in four situations outlined below. (It will be remembered that the retrospective effect of the FA 2022 changes is essentially limited to assessments of tax charges falling in those four bulleted categories.)

Each situation turns on the point having emerged in each case on or before 30 June 2021. The relevance of the 30 June 2021 cut-off date is that that was when the Upper Tribunal gave its decision in *Wilkes*. The purpose of the retrospection is to ensure that the benefit of the *Wilkes* argument is limited to those taxpayers who were sufficiently clued up (or advised of the argument) before the *Wilkes* point became more widely known.

To complicate matters, the legislation refers to "protected assessments". Such terminology might be thought to refer to those assessments that are protected *from* the retrospective effect of the FA 2022 changes. However, on closer inspection, it can be seen that a "protected assessment" is one that HMRC have managed to bring retrospectively within the scope of the new statutory wording (i.e. where HMRC have protected *their* position).

Law: FA 2022, s. 97(3)-(4)

Cases: *HMRC v Wilkes* [2021] UKUT 150 (TCC); *HMRC v Wilkes* EWCA Civ 1612

Situation 1 – Wilkes argument raised on or before 30 June 2021

The first category of case excused from the retrospective nature of the changes is where each of the following conditions is met:

- an appeal was notified to HMRC in writing on or before 30 June 2021;
- an issue in the appeal was the validity of the assessment because s. 29(1)(a) (i.e. the former wording) was not met; and
- that issue had been raised on or before 30 June 2021, either by the taxpayer or in a decision given by the tribunal.

This represents the paradigm situation, with the other situations being a variation of the theme.

It should be noted that a case might come within the terms of this situation even if the taxpayer had not expressly mentioned any of the arguments that have so far prevailed in *Wilkes*: all that is necessary is that there must be a ground of appeal that asserts that there has been no valid discovery because of non-satisfaction of s. 29(1)(a). In all likelihood, however, there will be very few cases where a taxpayer has raised non-satisfaction of s. 29(1)(a) without having in mind the *Wilkes* arguments. But it is not impossible, particularly if the case had been held up as a result of the *Tooth* litigation where there would also be a challenge to the existence of a valid discovery.

Law: FA 2022, s. 97(5), (9)

Cases: *HMRC v Tooth* [2021] UKSC 17; *HMRC v Wilkes* [2022] EWCA Civ 1612

Situation 2 – case paused before 27 October 2021

The second category of case excused from the retrospective nature of the changes is where each of the following conditions is met:

- an appeal was notified to HMRC in writing on or before 30 June 2021;
- the appeal was the subject of a temporary pause which occurred before 27 October 2021; and
- it is reasonable to conclude that the temporary pausing of the appeal occurred (wholly or partly) on the basis that the validity of the assessment for non-satisfaction of s. 29(1)(a) is, or might be, relevant to the determination of the appeal.

The significance of the 27 October 2021 date is that that is when the Budget took place and when the proposed change in the law was first announced.

A temporary pause is defined as either:

- a stay of the appeal by the tribunal;
- an agreement by the parties to stay the appeal; or
- a written notification by HMRC to the taxpayer that work on the case has been suspended pending the determination of another appeal, as identified to the taxpayer.

In *Ashe*, the taxpayer had appealed against a discovery assessment prior to 30 June 2021 and was about to embark upon the internal review process when he was told by HMRC in early October 2021 that all HICBC compliance activity was being put on hold. The tribunal considered that it would be reasonable to conclude that awaiting the outcome of the *Wilkes* case was at least a part of the reason for that pause. As a result, the retrospective change of the legislation did not apply to Mr Ashe's case.

Law: FA 2022, s. 97(6), (8), (9)
Case: *Ashe v HMRC* [2023] UKFTT 538 (TC)

Situation 3 – late appeals but Wilkes argument raised on or before 30 June 2021

The third category of case excused from the retrospective nature of the changes is a variant of situation 1 in cases where the appeal was made late and after 30 June 2021. It applies if each of the following conditions is met:

- an appeal was notified to HMRC in writing after 30 June 2021;

- the notice of appeal was given late (but allowed under TMA 1970, s. 49);

- a request in writing was made to HMRC on or before 30 June 2021 seeking HMRC's agreement to the notice being given late;

- an issue in the appeal was the validity of the assessment because s. 29(1)(a) (i.e. the former wording) was not met; and

- that issue had been raised on or before 30 June 2021, either by the taxpayer or in a decision given by the tribunal.

In the actual statute, this situation is described by deeming certain appeals made after 30 June to have been made on or before 30 June 2021.

Law: TMA 1970, s. 49; FA 2022, s. 97(5), (7), (9)

Situation 4 – late appeals and case paused before 27 October 2021

The final category of case excused from the retrospective nature of the changes is one where there is a late appeal, but the case was nevertheless stayed before 27 October 2021. It applies if each of the following conditions is met:

- an appeal was notified to HMRC in writing after 30 June 2021;

- the notice of appeal was given late (but allowed under TMA 1970, s. 49);

- a request in writing was made to HMRC on or before 30 June 2021 seeking HMRC's agreement to the notice being given late;

- the appeal was the subject of a temporary pause which occurred before 27 October 2021; and

- it is reasonable to conclude that the temporary pausing of the appeal occurred (wholly or partly) on the basis that the

> validity of the assessment for non-satisfaction of s. 29(1)(a) is, or might be, relevant to the determination of the appeal.

The definition of "temporary pause" follows that in relation to situation 2.

Law: FA 2022, s. 97(6), (7), (8), (9)

A case at the margins

In the case of *Kensall*, the taxpayer had been misinformed by HMRC about the prospects of any potential appeal and, therefore, he did not initially appeal against the HICBC assessment (although he did appeal against the corresponding penalties). When he learned of the potential *Wilkes* argument, the taxpayer then made an application for a late appeal.

Had he not been so misled by HMRC, the taxpayer would have made a timely appeal and fallen within situation 1. However, not only did the taxpayer fall outside the scope of situation 1, he also failed to meet the strict statutory conditions set out in respect of the other three situations.

The tribunal felt constrained to dismiss his appeal. However, it recognised that the taxpayer's inability to succeed was down to HMRC's conduct and the tribunal gave a strong hint that HMRC should exercise their discretion and waive the HICBC.

Case: *Kensall v HMRC* [2023] UKFTT 11 (TC)

3.9 Staleness

3.9.1 Introduction

As noted at **3.3.3** and **3.4.1**, the word "discover" implies the need for something that takes an officer from one side of the threshold (not knowing of the under-assessment) to the other (believing that such an under-assessment has occurred).

However, a string of decisions in the Upper Tribunal and the Court of Appeal suggested that there is a further aspect of this need for something new; according to that case law, an assessment would not be valid unless the discovery which underlies it had remained sufficiently fresh. In other words, an officer cannot simply sit on a discovery and choose to make the formal assessment at some later date.

The relevance of the point is that there can be occasions in which HMRC fail to act with sufficient alacrity to a perceived under-assessment. Given the potential unfairness to taxpayers of HMRC simply sitting on a discovery (especially if evidence is going to be harder to obtain as a result of any delays), it behoves them to act sufficiently swiftly and to notify the taxpayer of the potential dispute as early as can reasonably be expected.

This line of argument was finally killed off in mid-2021 by the Supreme Court's decision in *Tooth*. However, in the meantime, a body of case law had developed identifying when a delay between the discovery and the assessment would be appropriate. This is not entirely academic because the Supreme Court made clear that unreasonable delays could still lead to a discovery assessment being quashed on public law grounds.

Case: *HMRC v Tooth* [2021] UKSC 17

3.9.2   The earlier case law

In *Cenlon*, the broad meaning of discovery was summarised as follows:

> "... the words are apt to include *any* case in which for any reason it newly appears that the taxpayer has been undercharged ..."

In *Corbally-Stourton*, the Special Commissioner (when summarising the principles behind discovery assessments) noted the following:

> "There is one other aspect of the word 'discover' to which I should refer. This arises from *Cenlon Finance Co Ltd v Ellwood* to which I was referred by Miss Simler [Counsel for HMRC]: a 'discovery' is something newly arising, not something stale and old. The conclusion that it is probable that there is an insufficiency must be one which newly arises (from fresh facts or a new view of the law or otherwise)."

This was followed by the case of *Charlton*, where it was submitted (on behalf of the taxpayers) that one single officer reaching a conclusion which had been previously reached by other officers looking at similar cases would not qualify as a discovery, as any discovery would by then have become stale. This particular submission was not accepted by the Upper Tribunal, on the basis that there had been a fresh discovery so far as the relevant taxpayers were concerned. Nevertheless, the Upper Tribunal did accept the principle that staleness can defeat a discovery. As the tribunal held:

> "The requirement for newness does not relate to the reason for the conclusion reached by the officer, but to the conclusion itself. If an officer has concluded that a discovery assessment should be issued, but for some reason the assessment is not made within a reasonable period after that conclusion is reached, it might, depending on the circumstances, be the case that the conclusion would lose its essential newness by the time of the actual assessment."

Furthermore, the tribunal recognised that one officer (for whom a discovery is now stale) passing the file to another officer might not have the effect of refreshing the discovery:

> "Without deciding the matter, we can certainly envisage an argument that the passing of a file from one HMRC officer to another could not have the effect of refreshing a conclusion that was no longer new. But that does not depend on something new being discovered by reference to HMRC's collective knowledge. It is solely concerned with the newness of the conclusion."

Similarly, the principles were implicit in the Upper Tribunal's decision in *Sanderson*. However, there, the tribunal concluded that a discovery had been validly made because the officer only belatedly realised that the taxpayer had under-assessed his tax – the fact that the officer had all the necessary information in his files (and the proverbial penny had simply not dropped) was insufficient to deem the officer from having discovered the point any earlier. Had the discovery been made at that earlier time, there was a risk that the delayed assessment would have been rendered invalid by reason of staleness.

Cases: *Cenlon Finance Co Ltd v Ellwood* (1962) 40 TC 176; *Corbally-Stourton v HMRC* (2008) Sp C 692; *HMRC v Charlton (and others)* [2012] UKUT 770 (TCC); *Sanderson v HMRC* [2013] UKUT 623 (TCC)

3.9.3   The challenges to the principle

Despite those two cases in the Upper Tribunal positively addressing the question of staleness, HMRC started to argue late in 2015 that the Upper Tribunal's comments in *Charlton* were *obiter* (and therefore not binding) and, furthermore, that they were wrong.

On the first two occasions (*Pepper* and *Gakhal*), HMRC's submissions were accepted at face value, although it is noteworthy that in both cases the FTT's own findings were *obiter*.

The tribunal considered the matter more fully in the case of *Miesegaes*. However, the author respectfully considers that the tribunal erred both in its analysis of *Charlton* and in its approach to the need for something new to support a discovery.

The effect of each of these three decisions was simply that HMRC can make discovery assessments at any time (subject only to the statutory time limits), irrespective of any delay between the time when the necessary discovery was made and the assessment itself. In other words, the discovery need no longer be new. However, this view was subsequently superseded by a further decision of the Upper Tribunal (see **3.9.4** below).

Cases: *HMRC v Charlton (and others)* [2012] UKUT 770 (TCC); *Pepper v National Crime Agency* [2015] UKFTT 615 (TC); *Gakhal v HMRC* [2016] UKFTT 356 (TC); *Miesegaes v HMRC* [2016] UKFTT 375 (TC)

3.9.4   The Upper Tribunal upholding the staleness concept

The point was then fully argued and discussed in the Upper Tribunal case of *Pattullo*. The tribunal concluded that a discovery assessment can be defeated if the discovery is stale by the time that the assessment is made:

> "So far as concerns the question of law, namely whether any discovery under s 29(1) has to be acted upon while it remains fresh (or before it becomes stale), I prefer the submissions for the taxpayer. Quite apart from the support given to this submission by the passages in *Charlton* and *Corbally-Stourton* to which I have referred, which are highly persuasive, the requirement for the discovery to be acted upon while it remains fresh appears to me to arise on the natural meaning of s 29(1) itself. ... It would, to my mind, be absurd to contemplate

that, having made a discovery of the sort specified in s 29(1), HMRC could in effect just sit on it and do nothing for a number of years before making an assessment just before the end of the limitation period specified in s 34(1)."

Supportive statements were then given by the Upper Tribunal in *Tooth* although the case was not ultimately decided on the point. However, the point was reinforced by the Court of Appeal in HMRC's further appeal in that case.

Cases: *HMRC v Charlton (and others)* [2012] UKUT 770 (TCC); *Pattullo v HMRC* [2016] UKUT 270 (TCC); *Tooth v HMRC* [2016] UKFTT 723 (TC); *HMRC v Tooth* [2019] EWCA Civ 826

3.9.5   *The Supreme Court finally resolving the issue*

However, by the time that the *Tooth* case reached the Supreme Court, the judiciary took a different view. Whereas the Upper Tribunal in *Pattullo* had considered that the idea that a discovery had to remain fresh "appears ... to arise *on the natural meaning* of s 29(1) itself", the Supreme Court considered that such an interpretation was in fact "unsustainable as a matter of ordinary language".

It concluded that, so far as the statutory test was concerned (and therefore the tribunal's jurisdiction), it was necessary only for HMRC to prove that the officer making the assessment believes the previously assessed tax to be insufficient: it does not matter when the officer first formed that belief nor how many other officers had previously formed that belief.

Pending the Supreme Court's decision, a number of cases had been waiting in the wings as they turned on the question of staleness. In the main, they have now been disposed of with little fanfare in the light of *Tooth*. However, in *Harrison*, the taxpayer attempted to argue that the concept of staleness was not quite dead, but "merely resting". That argument was unequivocally rejected by the Upper Tribunal which, continuing the terminology from the TV series of *Monty Python*, declared the concept as "deceased". Even though the commentary in *Tooth* was, technically, *obiter dicta* and not a part of the Supreme Court's *ratio decidendi* (as HMRC's appeal had already failed on another ground), it was sufficiently definitive as to be binding.

In short, staleness is no longer arguable but it has left a legacy which might yet live on. (For completeness, however, following an announcement by the House of Lords in 1966, which has been adopted by the Supreme Court, it remains possible for the Supreme Court to depart from an earlier decision "when it appears right to do so". That is definitely not something that should ordinarily be expected.)

Cases: *HMRC v Tooth* [2021] UKSC 17; *Harrison v HMRC* [2023] UKUT 38 (TC)

Guidance: House of Lords *Practice Statement* 26 July 1966, [1966] 1 WLR 1234

3.9.6   *Can there still be unacceptable delays?*

Subject to the remote possibility of the matter being re-litigated, the concept of staleness is no longer one that applies in the context of discovery assessments.

However, and despite concluding that a discovery did not have to remain "fresh" by the time the assessment was made, the Supreme Court in *Tooth* made it clear that HMRC officers were still required to act reasonably once making a discovery. Thus, for example, in the case of an officer in 2024 discovering an under-assessment in relation to the 2020-21 tax year in circumstances where a 20-year time limit was available, the officer cannot simply say nothing for (say) a further 15 years and then issue the assessment, pointing only to the statutory time limits.

Accepting HMRC's arguments, the Supreme Court noted:

> "where the statutory discovery condition in section 29(1) is satisfied, an officer or the Board has a discretion whether to issue an assessment ("may ... make an assessment") and they must act in accordance with ordinary principles of public law in deciding whether to do so. So, for example, they must act rationally, must not abuse their powers and may be required to respect any legitimate expectation which they have created. If they fail to do so, the taxpayer may seek relief in judicial review proceedings."

The Supreme Court declined (quite properly) to define the boundary between acceptable and unacceptable behaviour. However, it did note that HMRC had accepted that:

"depending on the circumstances, a deliberate decision not to assess promptly might amount to irrationality which might in turn provide the basis for a remedy."

Even that, however, was not unequivocal given the inclusion of two qualifications: "depending on the circumstances" and "might". Furthermore, the Supreme Court was not strictly agreeing with the position but was merely reporting what HMRC had conceded. Nevertheless, the author considers that the Supreme Court can fairly be assumed to have agreed that HMRC's (limited) concession was fair.

Case: *HMRC v Tooth* [2021] UKSC 17

3.9.7   Previous examples of acceptable and unacceptable delays

It is currently too soon to know how such judicial review claims might fare. Furthermore, there is a risk that the courts will consider that not acting on a discovery in a sufficiently prompt manner, so as to let it go stale, will not in itself amount to conduct that is irrational.

On the other hand, the practical application of the staleness concept did evolve so as to strike a fair balance between HMRC and taxpayers. Accordingly, it is at least possible that, perhaps with some modification, a similar approach would be taken by the courts in any future judicial review challenge.

At present, therefore, it is considered that the previous case law decisions will continue to be illustrative.

In any event, it has always been quite clear that an officer is not required to make an assessment the instant that a discovery is made. Ultimately, it is down to what is reasonable on the facts of any particular case. For example, in *Pattullo*, the Upper Tribunal accepted the submissions made by the author as follows:

"Mr Gordon was at pains to emphasise that HMRC need not make an assessment immediately upon making a discovery in terms of s 29(1). It would be sufficient, he submitted, for HMRC to notify the taxpayer of its discovery in the expectation that matters could be resolved without the need for a formal assessment. In each case the question whether the discovery had been kept "fresh" would turn on its particular facts. It would only be in the most exceptional of cases, he said, that the conduct of HMRC, for example their inaction, would result in the discovery losing its required "newness" by the time that an assessment was made."

In *Charlton*, it was considered appropriate to wait a few months pending the decision of the Supreme Court in another case as to whether or not permission to appeal would be granted. Similarly, in *Hayes*, the tribunal made the following observations:

"We do not think that a delay of six months is sufficient to mean that the discovery has lost its 'newness' such as to be stale. In any event, we conclude that even if (which we very much doubt) a delay of six months can ever justify a finding of staleness, it cannot do so in this case. HMRC did not simply sit on their hands during the period between the discovery and the issuing of the first assessment; HMRC engaged with Mr Hayes including with a view to settlement."

On the other hand, in *Pattullo*, where the taxpayer had not been told of any discovery (and, indeed, the relevant officer had claimed to be incapable of making a discovery), it was held that on the assumption that the actual discovery had been made at the time being argued for by the taxpayer, "the passage of some 18 months or more would, in the circumstances of this case, have made the discovery stale and incapable of justifying the assessment made".

Conversely, in *Hicks*, it was suggested that a "delay of at most 9 months" was not sufficient to render a discovery stale, particularly as "HMRC were not sitting on their hands" in the interim.

It should be noted, however, that the FTT in *Hicks* appears to have ignored the possibility that the discovery might have been made by a different officer, at an earlier time, with the conclusion that passing the file to a new officer can potentially reset the clock. Such a conclusion appears to be inconsistent with the view expressed in *Charlton* as summarised at **3.9.2** above. (In the Upper Tribunal, the matter did not arise because the tribunal considered that there was inadequate evidence to support the existence of the earlier discovery.)

In *Stirling*, the tribunal noted:

> "The decisions in the Upper Tribunal all make clear that each case turns on its own particular facts. On the facts of this case, we do not consider that 10 months was too long. This is always a matter of fact and degree, but it is still significantly less than the 18 months which Lord Glennie would have considered, 'on any view', too long."

This was mirrored in *Royal Bank of Canada* when the delay was "some 15-16 months". The tribunal explain its decision thus:

> "As was made clear in *Pattullo*, however, there is no single period of delay that can simply be mapped across from one case to another to establish staleness – Lord Glennie was keen to make it clear that his 18 month statement was specific to the circumstances of that case. Counsel for the taxpayer in that case had ... acknowledged that a discovery could be prevented from going stale by 'notification being given to the taxpayer of the discovery in the expectation that matters could be resolved without the need for a formal assessment to be made'. I consider that acknowledgment to have been correct and that this is just such a case."

In *Gordon*, however, the delay was three years and that was too long.

In *Beagles*, the Upper Tribunal considered that merely notifying a taxpayer of the fact of a discovery was not on its own sufficient to keep the discovery fresh:

> "if a concept of staleness is to have any meaning, HMRC cannot use a notification like that to justify leaving a matter open without taking any action for an unlimited period ... If the discovery was to retain its quality of "newness" notwithstanding that delay, it was incumbent upon HMRC to take further steps in order to preserve that quality in the period between the making of the discovery and the issue of the assessment ..."

In *Oriel*, the FTT considered that a discovery had gone stale in a situation where HMRC had first given effect to the discovery by way of amendment, rather than assessment. Although the taxpayer challenged the legality of the amendment, the parties agreed to wait until the outcome of a similar case. That process took nearly three years. HMRC argued that they were precluded from issuing a discovery assessment in the interim as that would have been inconsistent with their view that an amendment was valid. However, the tribunal held that there was no restriction on an assessment being issued 'in the alternative'; ultimately, by waiting, HMRC's discovery had become stale.

In *Norton*, the tribunal was dealing with a delay of nine months, which the tribunal considered could have been sufficient to let the discovery go stale. However, unlike the silence identified in *Beagles*, the officer had spent the time discussing the matter with the taxpayer's adviser. Rather than doing nothing, the officer:

> "... took steps to confirm his analysis in response to [the taxpayer's accountants'] arguments, chased for replies and further information and pursued settlement negotiations. This was not a case [where] the taxpayer was prejudiced or could have been prejudiced by delay on the part of HMRC. His discovery did not go stale."

As the tribunal remarked in *Odey*:

> "A discovery should not be regarded as losing its 'essential newness' where, in the period before the assessment is issued, there are on-going active discussions/correspondence between the parties in relation to the tax issue in question such that the taxpayer cannot be in any doubt that HMRC intend to issue it. 'Staleness' is about HMRC not being able just to sit on their hands when they could act on their discovery. This principle is not intended to discourage full enquiries, attempts to settle or to provide a windfall to a taxpayer where an enquiry has been slow due to the actions of the taxpayer and information has been provided very gradually."

The author does consider that, even if the courts do generally follow the tribunals' previous views on staleness when considering the boundaries of irrationality, the preceding cases should not be assumed to be slavishly followed. In particular, when applying the concept of staleness, a tribunal would generally focus on when the discovery was first made and whether it was kept fresh in the interim. In any potential judicial review claim, a court is likely to be just as interested in understanding the reasons for the intervening delay when deciding whether HMRC's later decision to make the assessment is to be treated as unlawful.

Cases: *HMRC v Charlton (and others)* [2012] UKUT 770 (TCC); *Pattullo v HMRC* [2016] UKUT 270 (TCC); *Hicks v HMRC* [2018] UKFTT 22 (TC); *Stirling Jewellers (Dudley) Ltd v HMRC* [2019] UKFTT 44 (TC); *Gordon v HMRC* [2018] UKFTT 307 (TC); *Beagles v HMRC* [2018] UKUT 380 (TCC); *Oriel Developments Ltd v HMRC* [2019] UKFTT 503 (TC); *HMRC v Hicks* [2020] UKUT 12 (TCC); *Hayes v HMRC* [2020] UKFTT 266 (TC); *Royal Bank of Canada v HMRC* [2020] UKFTT 267 (TC); *Norton v HMRC* [2020] UKFTT 503 (TC); *Odey Asset Management LLP v HMRC* [2021] UKFTT 31 (TC); *HMRC v Tooth* [2021] UKSC 17

3.9.8   Challenging an irrational delay

The Supreme Court in *Tooth* implicitly accepted HMRC's suggestion that an irrational delay to making an assessment could be the subject of a judicial review. The author does not demur from that suggestion. However, evolving case law in other contexts raises the possibility that such public law arguments might also (or perhaps instead) be deployed in the tribunal as part of an appeal.

The latest decision supporting such a prospect (albeit in the VAT context) is the Upper Tribunal's decision in *KSM*. However, it should be noted that HMRC's firm view is that public law arguments should not be entertained otherwise than in the course of judicial review.

For a fuller discussion of these issues, see the author's *Tax Appeals*, also available from Claritax Books.

Case: *KSM Henryk Zeman SP Z.o.o v HMRC* [2021] UKUT 182 (TCC)

4. Additional safeguards when a tax return has been made

4.1 Introduction

In cases where the taxpayer has submitted a tax return for the relevant tax year, the discovery rules contain additional protections for the taxpayer. These protections were introduced as part of a balanced package of measures when self-assessment was introduced. On the one hand, taxpayers were exposed to a 12-month enquiry window, meaning that there was a year-long risk of their tax return being looked at. On the other hand, once the risk of an enquiry had passed, taxpayers are entitled to a sense of finality. As a result, HMRC's right to revisit the return and issue a discovery assessment is subject to additional restrictions.

Accordingly, as well as showing that they have made a discovery (see **Chapter 3** above) HMRC will need to satisfy at least one of two additional procedural conditions for any discovery assessment to be valid.

Those conditions are that:

- the original under-assessment was attributable to the careless or deliberate conduct of the taxpayer (or a person acting on the taxpayer's behalf); or
- the tax return (and other documentation deemed to be before a "hypothetical tax officer") would not have been sufficient to alert the hypothetical officer to the under-assessment.

Those two alternative conditions are discussed in **Chapters 5** and **6** below.

Law: TMA 1970, s. 29(3)

4.2 Submitting a return

4.2.1 Statutory position

The statute makes it clear that the return must be a self-assessment return (as opposed to a VAT return, say) under TMA 1970, s. 8

(individuals) or 8A (trustees), which has been both "made and delivered".

Furthermore, that return must be made in respect of the same tax year as that in relation to which the assessment is made.

In addition, this further protection applies only if the taxpayer's return was made by the taxpayer in the same capacity as that in which the taxpayer is now being assessed. Therefore, it will be of no help to a taxpayer who (as the trustee of a settlement) has made a trust return for a particular tax year and who is now being assessed personally.

Law: TMA 1970, s. 29(3)

4.2.2   Unsolicited returns

Although the vast majority of cases involve taxpayers who have indeed made returns, three FTT decisions in *Bloomsbury*, *Revell* and *Patel* mean that this should not be taken for granted. In particular, each case concluded (contrary to HMRC's own practice) that unsolicited tax returns (i.e. those for which there had been no prior notice served by HMRC requiring a return) did not constitute tax returns.

Although those cases were not concerned with the procedural conditions for a discovery assessment, the tribunal's conclusions in them could have allowed HMRC to side-step the additional safeguards available to those taxpayers who had submitted a return. However, from the introduction of the TMA, s. 12D (as inserted by FA 2019), unsolicited returns have been legitimised with retrospective effect so as to protect taxpayers from this risk.

Law: TMA 1970, s. 12D

Cases: *Bloomsbury Verlag GmbH v HMRC* [2015] UKFTT 660 (TC); *Revell v HMRC* [2016] UKFTT 97 (TC); *Patel v HMRC* [2018] UKFTT 185 (TC)

4.2.3   Late returns

In *Poulter*, it was suggested that a taxpayer lost the protection of s. 29(3) if the tax return was submitted late, on the basis that the tax return could no longer be said to have been made "under section 8" if it breached the time limits specified in that section.

The author respectfully considers that to represent a misreading of s. 29(3). The subsection refers to the nature of the return and not its timing.

It should be noted that a similarly restrictive reading was also suggested in the case of *Barrett*. However, that concerned a different statutory provision where the requirement was for the taxpayer to have made a return "in accordance with" rather than merely "under" s. 8.

Law: TMA 1970, s. 29(3)

Cases: *Poulter v HMRC* [2012] UKFTT 670 (TC); *Barrett v HMRC* [2015] UKFTT 329 (TC)

4.3 Other taxes

4.3.1 Corporation tax

The equivalent provisions are found in FA 1998, Sch. 18, para. 43.

4.3.2 SDLT

The equivalent provisions are found in FA 2003, Sch. 10, para. 30(2).

4.3.3 ATED

The equivalent provisions are found in FA 2013, Sch. 33, para. 24(2).

4.3.4 Digital services tax

The equivalent provisions are found in FA 2020, Sch. 8, para. 20(1).

4.3.5 Public interest business protection tax

The equivalent provisions are found in FA 2022, Sch. 10, para. 18(2).

4.3.6 Multinational top-up tax

The equivalent provisions are found in F(No. 2)A 2023, Sch. 14, para. 28.

5. Careless or deliberate conduct

5.1 Introduction

As noted in **Chapter 4**, two additional conditions apply in cases where a taxpayer has submitted a return for the relevant period. HMRC need to show that at least one of those conditions is satisfied.

This Chapter considers the first of those two conditions. The alternative condition is discussed in **Chapter 6** below.

Law: TMA 1970, s. 29(3)

5.2 The "careless or deliberate" test

5.2.1 Historical background

For assessments made before 1 April 2010, the statutory test turned on "fraudulent or negligent conduct". In practice, it is often assumed that the net effect of the statute is unchanged. Nevertheless, case law dealing with the earlier wording should be applied with increasing care, as the new statutory test is becoming more established.

Law: TMA 1970, s. 29(4)

5.2.2 Transitional rule

There is a transitional rule which theoretically applies in a few cases for some assessments made between 1 April 2010 and 31 March 2012.

The effect of that transitional rule is to continue to apply the old "fraudulent or negligent" test in cases where HMRC delayed giving a notice to file a tax return for more than a year after the end of the relevant tax year.

However, it is considered that the transitional rule in fact has no practical effect because it contains a further provision which disapplies the transitional rule in cases where the conditions for a discovery are met. Indeed, it is not believed that any cases have turned on the transitional rule in the thirteen plus years following its introduction.

In the author's opinion, the transitional rule may therefore be ignored for these purposes.

Law: SI 2009/403, art. 2(2), 10

5.2.3 Scope of present rule

For all assessments made on or after 1 April 2010 (except those exceptional cases (if any) covered by the transitional rule in **5.2.2** above), the new "careless or deliberate" test applies.

That is the case even if the tax year governed by the assessment predates April 2010. For those earlier years, there is a further transitional rule governing time limits (see **8.3** below).

5.3 The statutory test

5.3.1 The causal connection

Great care must be taken when facing an allegation by HMRC of "careless or deliberate conduct". The statute is very clear in that it requires "the situation" (being the subject matter of the discovery – i.e. the perceived loss of tax) to have been "brought about carelessly or deliberately by the taxpayer or a person acting on his behalf".

In other words, it is not sufficient for HMRC to assert (as they often do) simply that there has been (say) careless conduct. For example, the author has heard it suggested that the required carelessness occurred when the taxpayer submitted his tax return after the due date. If the discovery assessment is to be valid, HMRC must show that the under-assessment (or excessive claim for relief etc.) was itself attributable to the culpable conduct complained of.

Furthermore, as illustrated by the *Hargreaves* case, a taxpayer's careless failure to seek advice when completing the tax return is not necessarily sufficient to justify a discovery assessment. As the Upper Tribunal held, it is also necessary for HMRC to demonstrate that such advice would have led to more tax being assessed:

> "[I]f [the advisers] could legitimately (i.e. non-negligently) have advised Mr Hargreaves that, despite the change in circumstances, it would still be appropriate for him to submit the Return with a claim to be non-resident, that would support

Mr Hargreaves' argument that the Situation was not attributable to the negligence found against him ..."

Case: *HMRC v Hargreaves* [2022] UKUT 34 (TCC)
Law: TMA 1970, s. 29(4)

5.3.2   *Whose conduct?*

As noted in the previous paragraphs, HMRC can satisfy the test in s. 29(4) by pointing to the conduct of a person other than the taxpayer. This distinguishes the discovery rules from those (otherwise similar) rules governing penalties, as the latter generally turn on the culpability of the actual taxpayer.

In *Clixby*, a case concerning an allegation of fraud, Cross J considered it irrelevant that the taxpayer was not privy to the adviser's dishonest conduct. In other words, the taxpayer might be entirely innocent of any inappropriate conduct but is still exposed to a discovery assessment.

However, in *McCumiskey*, the fraudulent adviser had not been properly authorised by the taxpayer. Accordingly, the adviser's actions did not render the taxpayer liable to the discovery assessment. (Indeed, the tribunal considered that the lack of authority granted to the fraudulent adviser meant that the original inadequate "return" had not actually been made by the taxpayer, meaning that there was (in that case) nothing to discover.) A similar result was reached in *Robson*.

The statutory provision refers to "a person acting on his behalf". This does not simply mean any person who might have contributed to the figures that made up a tax return. Instead, the wording was judicially defined in *Taube* as follows:

"In our view, the expression 'person acting on ... behalf' is not apt to describe a mere adviser who only provides advice to the taxpayer or to someone who is acting on the taxpayer's behalf. In our judgement the expression connotes a person who takes steps that the taxpayer himself could take, or would otherwise be responsible for taking. Such steps will commonly include steps involving third parties, but will not necessarily do so. Examples would in our view include completing a return, filing a return, entering into correspondence with HMRC, providing documents and information to HMRC and seeking external advice as to the legal and tax position of the taxpayer. The person must represent, and not merely provide advice to, the taxpayer."

Thus, there can be a number of instances where an error on a tax return is as a direct result of careless or deliberate conduct, yet that fact alone should not to be sufficient to justify a discovery assessment. Such instances will include:

- a bank which mis-states the interest received by a taxpayer on a bank account; or
- a tax avoidance specialist who provides a scheme which the taxpayer enters into but which later proves to be ineffective.

Of course, any subsequent carelessness or deliberate conduct by the taxpayer personally (or by the taxpayer's agent), which also contributes to the error on the tax return, could render the taxpayer liable for a discovery assessment.

It should be noted that, in *Atherton*, the FTT expressed difficulties in *obiter dicta* with the views expressed in *Taube*. However, the matter was finally resolved by the Upper Tribunal in *Hicks* which expressly endorsed the *Taube* formulation.

In *Field*, a case concerning SDLT and the situation after the relevant returns had been submitted but where the legislation was then retroactively changed, the tribunal applied the *Hicks* approach and considered that advisers who corresponded with HMRC and advised the taxpayers that there was no need to amend their returns were acting on the taxpayers' behalf.

Law: TMA 1970, s. 29(4)

Cases: *Clixby v Pountney (HM Inspector of Taxes)* (1967) 44 TC 515; *Trustees of the Bessie Taube Discretionary Settlement Trust v HMRC (and others)* [2010] UKFTT 473 (TC); *Atherton v HMRC* [2017] UKFTT 831 (TC); *HMRC v Hicks* [2020] UKUT 12 (TCC); *G C Field & Sons Ltd v HMRC* [2021] UKFTT 297 (TC); *McCumiskey v HMRC* [2022] UKFTT 128 (TC); *Robson v HMRC* [2023] UKFTT 226 (TC)

5.3.3   Practical issues

The statute provides the alternative "or" – *either* careless conduct *or* deliberate conduct will suffice. Of course, if HMRC were able to show that both applied, that would be sufficient to justify a discovery assessment. Indeed, HMRC often make the assertion that a taxpayer's conduct was "at least careless" implying that it could have been more serious. On the other hand, there is an argument (which the author favours) that the two types of behaviour are mutually exclusive.

Furthermore, it is a fundamental principle of court practice that a party alleging serious conduct such as dishonesty, fraud or bad faith (and it is suggested that deliberate conduct falls within this category) should do so expressly and clearly (typically in a statement of case for the tribunal). See, for example, *Infinity*.

However, the Supreme Court in *Tooth* acknowledged that the statutory gloss to the meaning of deliberate (see **5.5.3** below) opens the way to conduct being classed as deliberate even though it falls well short of a deliberate under-declaration of tax, that might previously have been described as fraudulent. Accordingly, it remains to be seen whether this will pave the way to a more relaxed approach to how allegations are required to be made.

Furthermore, in practice, HMRC generally assume that there is a spectrum of behaviours, with deliberate conduct being at the more serious end, and with certain forms of recklessness bridging the two. Nevertheless, in *Daniel* (which concerned the earlier test of fraudulent or negligent conduct in the context of a taxpayer claiming to have been resident outside the UK), the tribunal made the following comments:

> "We also note the quite difficult point that in addressing the question of whether a claim to have been non-resident was negligent or not, there is arguably little middle ground between the claim having been tenable and honest, and the claim having been fraudulent. It is quite difficult to describe the circumstances where negligence is the apt expression to cover an Appellant's conduct. In other words if the claim is plainly honest, and also tenable (even though borderline) there should be no risk of negligence being established. If the taxpayer thinks and decides that there are doubts, and perhaps major doubts, and he files the return on the basis of a hope that HMRC will fail to open enquiries, then that conduct comes closer to fraud than negligence. And in this case, HMRC has never

> asserted fraud and we certainly do not suggest that the Appellant was fraudulent."

Similarly, in *Robson*, the tribunal said:

> "In my view carelessness connotes a different manner of behaviour to and is distinct from fraudulent conduct."

That was potentially significant because HMRC had based their case on assertions of carelessness. The tribunal considered that the behaviour of the firm preparing Mr Robson's tax return had gone "further than that", with the tribunal effectively accepting (without expressly saying) that the firm had completed the returns fraudulently. However, as deliberate conduct was not a part of HMRC's case, the tribunal did not need to make any express findings on that alternative basis.

For the purposes of this Chapter, the two tests will be considered discretely.

Cases: *Daniel v HMRC* [2014] UKFTT 173 (TC); *HMRC v Infinity Distribution Ltd (in administration)* [2016] EWCA Civ 1014; *HMRC v Tooth* [2021] UKSC 17; *Robson v HMRC* [2023] UKFTT 226 (TC).

5.4 Careless conduct

5.4.1 The statutory definition

Although tribunals often try to apply the normal meaning of the term (as was necessary under the previous equivalent test for negligence), there is in fact a statutory definition of careless conduct. It provides as follows:

> "a loss of tax or a situation is brought about carelessly by a person if the person fails to take reasonable care to avoid bringing about that loss or situation."

As yet, however, there is no case law which identifies exactly whether this is a complete definition of "carelessly" or whether it simply extends the normal meaning the word to cover cases where there has been a failure to take reasonable care. In the author's opinion, the statute is providing a complete definition. However, in *Hicks*, the Upper Tribunal considered that s. 118(5) did no more than ensure that "careless can take the form of omissions as well as positive acts". It added by saying that what amounts to carelessness "involves a factual assessment having regard to all the relevant circumstances of the case".

Nevertheless, it is considered that a taxpayer can disprove an assertion of careless conduct by demonstrating that he in fact took reasonable care (for example, by instructing a suitably qualified adviser). It must be remembered, however, that carelessness by the adviser will not save the taxpayer from a discovery assessment. As to where the burden of proof lies with regard to this test, see **9.3.3** below.

However, it is not sufficient for a taxpayer to point only to the steps taken to ensure that the return was correct when submitted. This is because the statute definitely extends the meaning of carelessness to certain failings that occur at a later stage.

In particular, carelessness will be deemed to have occurred if the taxpayer:

- learns that information previously provided to HMRC was in fact inaccurate; and
- fails to take reasonable steps to inform HMRC.

In this case, it will be seen that only the taxpayer's knowledge is relevant in such cases – a professional adviser who learns of a previous error and who fails to do anything about it will not cause the taxpayer to be deemed to have been careless.

Furthermore, the use of the word "information" suggests that errors in calculating a taxpayer's tax liability will not themselves require correction under this rule. However, most if not all components of the tax computation will themselves turn on "information" and therefore should be corrected.

It is the author's view that taking "reasonable steps" includes asking a suitable adviser to notify HMRC on the taxpayer's behalf and also implies that the steps will be taken without unreasonable delay.

Law: TMA 1970, s. 118(5), (6)
Case: *HMRC v Hicks* [2020] UKUT 12 (TCC)

5.4.2   The case law

For many years, it was relatively common for parties (or even the tribunal) to refer to a 19th century authority (*Blyth*) on the meaning of negligence which stated:

> "Negligence is the omission to do something which a reasonable man, guided upon those considerations which ordinarily regulate the conduct of human affairs, would do, or doing something which a prudent and reasonable man would not do. The defendants might be liable for negligence, if, unintentionally, they omitted to do that which a prudent and reasonable person would have done, or did that which a person taking reasonable care would not have done."

Although the *Blyth* formulation has probably formed the basis of training manuals for decades (thereby affecting the approach taken both within and outside HMRC), the tribunal has since started to doubt its relevance in the context of tax statutes. For example, in *AB*, two very experienced Special Commissioners held:

> "the question whether a taxpayer has engaged in negligent conduct is a question of fact in each case. We should take the words of the statute as we find them and not try to articulate principles which could restrict the application of the statutory words. However, we accept that negligent conduct amounts to more than just being wrong or taking a different view from the Revenue."

The relevance of the *Blyth* test has been doubted further, specifically given the fact that the word "careless" now appears in the statutory test. For example, in *Berrier*, the tribunal remarked:

> "In that case [*Blyth*] the issue was whether damage sustained was by reason of the negligence of the waterworks company in not keeping their water pipes and equipment in proper order. The *Blyth* case is neither relevant nor binding on us as it concerns a different legal issue (negligence) and wholly different factual circumstances. We consider that reference to 19th century cases relating to negligence is misplaced in the context of the interpretation of "careless" in a statutory provision for tax penalties enacted by the *Finance Act* 2007. It is clear that in enacting the *Finance Act* 2007, Parliament

deliberately chose not to set the standard required in the preparation of documents by reference to "neglect" or "negligence" (the terms used previously in tax legislation), but instead by reference to carelessness."

Although *Berrier* itself involved penalties and therefore did not concern discovery assessments, the comments are apt.

Despite this, the above quotation from *Blyth* still appears in HMRC's manuals.

Cases: *Blyth v Birmingham Waterworks* (1856) 11 Ex 781; *AB (a firm) v HMRC* (2006) Sp C 572; *Berrier v HMRC* [2014] UKFTT 457 (TC)
Guidance: CH 53400

Subjective or objective carelessness

Some cases suggest that the test to be applied is entirely objective, in that a person's conduct is judged against a purely hypothetical standard. Therefore, a taxpayer is judged by reference to an average taxpayer; an adviser is similarly judged by reference to an average adviser. For example, in *Anderson*, the tribunal held:

> "The test to be applied, in my view, is to consider what a reasonable taxpayer, exercising reasonable diligence in the completion and submission of the return, would have done."

This was expressly endorsed by the Upper Tribunal in *Moore*.

However, most cases (e.g. *Hanson*) tend to qualify the above and apply the objective standards of reasonable conduct by reference to the taxpayer's (or the adviser's) own specific circumstances. Thus a taxpayer with specialist experience is expected to apply such experience. Similarly, in relation to persons acting on the taxpayer's behalf, a higher standard will be expected of a specialist than of a general practitioner.

It was this latter formulation that was implicitly endorsed by the Upper Tribunal in *Hicks*. It referred to the approach as follows:

> "what a reasonable and prudent taxpayer in the position of [the taxpayer] would have done, and what a reasonable and prudent accountant in the position of [the taxpayer's adviser] would have done in acting on behalf of [the taxpayer]. That test

had to take account of all the circumstances, including their characteristics and the relationship between them."

Cases: *Anderson v HMRC* [2009] UKFTT 258 (TC); *Moore v HMRC* [2011] UKUT 239 (TCC); *Hanson v HMRC* [2012] UKFTT 314 (TC); *HMRC v Hicks* [2020] UKUT 12 (TCC)

Carelessness and innocence

Rather unhelpfully, some tribunal decisions use certain non-statutory terms, such as "innocent", with different meanings. In some cases (an approach that the author personally prefers), the term "innocent" relates to conduct that is neither careless nor deliberate.

However, other cases (for example, *Anderson*) use the term "innocent" to mean not deliberate.

This confusion is sometimes exploited by HMRC and it is therefore important to understand precisely what is meant when such terms are being used.

Case: *Anderson v HMRC* [2009] UKFTT 258 (TC)

5.4.3   Causation

For the statutory test to be satisfied, it is necessary for the careless conduct to cause the loss of tax.

Some years ago, the author had seen an HMRC officer advance the argument that a tax return was late, that the lateness was a matter of carelessness and, therefore, any under-assessment on the (admittedly late) tax return was sufficiently careless to satisfy the statutory test. That, however, was an isolated case. Subject to that exception, it appears to have been generally accepted that there has to be a causal link between the asserted careless conduct and the loss of tax.

That was the position confirmed by the Upper Tribunal in *Bella Figura* (albeit in the context of the similarly worded provision governing time limits). As the Upper Tribunal put it (with emphasis as per the Upper Tribunal's own decision):

"[the statutory test] is concerned with the question of whether a failure to take reasonable care *causes* a loss of tax".

Notwithstanding that, the FTT in *Delphi* expressly concluded that the test of causation is not relevant. Instead, it held that:

> "the nexus required to be established is one of attribution in the sense that the inaccuracy can be accounted for by a mode of behaviour which is characterised as a failure to take reasonable care".

Thus, according to the FTT in *Delphi*, if there is some carelessness in the background, that is sufficient; it is not necessary for the actual loss of tax to have been caused by that carelessness. The author wishes to make clear that the FTT's decision in *Delphi* looks to be at odds with the legislation itself and previous practice and case law. Unless it is confirmed in a higher tribunal or court, it should be assumed that the *Delphi* decision is wrong.

Cases: *HMRC v Bella Figura Ltd* [2020] UKUT 120 (TCC); *Delphi Derivatives Ltd v HMRC* [2023] UKFTT 722 (TC)

5.4.4   Carelessness in practice

Generally

Essentially, the test is whether or not the taxpayer (or a person acting on the taxpayer's behalf) took reasonable care to avoid causing the loss of tax. As was said in *AB*, a taxpayer simply making a mistake is not enough.

It has generally been considered that a taxpayer obtaining professional advice should provide a full defence in virtually all cases. The possible exception would be where a taxpayer approaches an adviser who is quite clearly unsuited for the area in which advice is being sought – for example, to use an extreme and most unlikely scenario, a multi-national corporation seeking advice on a major corporate reconstruction from an adviser who professes to offer no more than payroll support.

Indeed, in *AB*, the Special Commissioners held:

> "We also accept that a taxpayer who takes proper and appropriate professional advice with a view to ensuring that his tax return is correct, and acts in accordance with that advice (if it is not obviously wrong), would not have engaged in negligent conduct."

Furthermore, in the penalty case of *Barrett* (which turned on the question of reasonable excuse, where the burden of proof lies on the taxpayer), the tribunal noted:

> "I do not agree that Mr Barrett's actions were unreasonable. In my view, the steps taken by Mr Barrett to employ an accountant who evidently held himself out as able to provide a comprehensive service, both as regards accounting and tax, for a small business such as that of Mr [Barrett], and in providing all relevant documentation to [his accountant], were the actions of a reasonable taxpayer in the position of Mr Barrett. Whilst Mr Barrett did not undertake any research in to [the accountant's] capabilities before appointing him, he was reasonably entitled to assume, from [the accountant's] acceptance of the appointment, that [the accountant] would be competent to deal with both the accounting and tax aspects of his business. I do not accept that such a reasonable taxpayer would necessarily have taken separate steps to inform himself, independently of his accountant, of his obligations to make returns under the CIS, whether by seeking a second opinion, or by consulting HMRC, or HMRC's published guidance, himself.
>
> The test is one of reasonableness. No higher (or lower) standard should be applied. The mere fact that something that could have been done has not been done does not of itself necessarily mean that an individual's conduct in failing to act in a particular way is to be regarded as unreasonable. It is a question of degree having regard to all the circumstances, including the particular circumstances of the individual taxpayer. There can be no universal rule; what might be considered an unreasonable failure on the part of one taxpayer in one set of circumstances might be regarded as not unreasonable in the case of another whose circumstances are different."

It is the author's firm view that a taxpayer who can show a reasonable excuse for an error will have a full defence against an assertion that he or she has been careless (i.e. failed to take reasonable care), where the burden of proof in fact falls on HMRC.

It is noteworthy that Mr Barrett actually had some previous knowledge of the CIS scheme and HMRC relied upon this to argue that this imposed a greater obligation on him to ensure compliance with the rules. However, the tribunal considered that, in the circumstances of the case, Mr Barrett's conduct could not be criticised as unreasonable – his previous knowledge was sufficiently divorced from his later mistakes.

Furthermore, the tribunal dispelled the myth that reasonable excuse is available only to taxpayers with more sophisticated affairs, who can be expected to need to rely upon the advice of specialists. As the tribunal held:

> "Nor do I consider that there can be any principled distinction between cases which involve complex or "arcane" provisions of tax law, and those which may be regarded as more commonplace. That is nothing more than one of the circumstances to be taken into account in the application of the objective standard."

It should be remembered that *Barrett* concerned penalties for non-compliance with the CIS and, in that context, unlike with discovery assessments, HMRC may not rely on the alleged carelessness of any person acting on the taxpayer's behalf.

In *Supaglazing*, the tribunal accepted that a genuine belief as to the tax position could not amount to carelessness because a view had been taken intentionally. However, that was subject to the proviso that the belief had to be reasonably held.

In *Belloul*, the tribunal applied and reversed the well-known *dicta* from *Nicholson* (see **9.3.2** below) in response to HMRC's assertion that a taxpayer had failed to observe certain guidance on HMRC's website. As the tribunal noted:

> "In my view it is not incumbent on the objectively reasonable taxpayer without notice of a change in tax law to go rummaging through all of HMRC's information on the off chance that there might be something which is hidden away in it which is relevant to his tax position."

In *Loughrey*, a case in which the taxpayer wrongly deducted his termination payment of £30,000 from the figure of pay in his P45 (not realising that that figure had already been adjusted to reflect the £30,000 exemption), the tribunal considered that the error was not due to carelessness. As the tribunal noted, Mr Loughrey had followed the online guidance given and there was no (obvious) indication that sometimes the P45 figure would already take the exemption into account. The tribunal also rejected the notion that Mr Loughrey (who had had no previous experience of filing a tax return) should have sought professional assistance for a task that did not appear to be particularly complicated and where HMRC's guidance did not suggest that additional advice might be needed.

In *Field*, a case which involved a retroactive change in the law to stop a particular avoidance scheme, the tribunal made the following comment:

> "Using the distinction in *Neal* [between basic ignorance of primary law and issues arising out of difficult questions of law], this is not a case of basic ignorance. The possibility that retrospective legislation might require you to revisit a transaction that had been returned under advice and disclosed is not something that a reasonable lay taxpayer would reasonably be expected to be aware of."

In *Kingdon*, the taxpayers were held to have "simply signed whatever [their former adviser] put in front of them". The FTT made it clear that they were entitled to take that approach, without being negligent (the case concerned the old test), but with an important caveat: "subject to checking, to the extent of their personal abilities".

In *Rizvi*, the tribunal concluded that the taxpayer's claims for EIS relief were not carelessly made, even though the taxpayer did not have the EIS3 forms that were an essential condition for the claims to have been made. The tribunal considered that requirement to be "a mechanical exercise which [at least in that case] it would be perfectly reasonable and prudent to leave to accountants". However, the accountants' own failure to allow a client to make a claim for EIS relief without making sure that the client held a valid EIS3 was described as "carelessness of a high order".

In *Altunis*, the FTT upheld an allegation of carelessness on the basis that the taxpayer had doubts as to the effectiveness of the avoidance scheme he had signed up to. Those doubts, according to the FTT, should have led him to take a second opinion and not rely on the promoters and the extracts of Counsel's opinion which the promoters provided to him.

In *Delphi*, a case about penalties but considering the same statutory wording, the FTT was addressing the argument that the erroneous professional advice relied upon by the taxpayer was not a defence to HMRC's assertion that the taxpayer had acted carelessly by not taking a second opinion. The taxpayer put forward the argument that, had any further opinion been sought, that opinion would have agreed with the initial advice given the widespread views in the tax profession at the time. The author is of the view that, had there been evidence to support that argument, that argument should have been an effective defence against the allegation of carelessness.

However, the FTT took the view that, for such an argument to succeed, the taxpayer would need to prove a prevailing practice (akin to that discussed at **7.2.4**). This is because the FTT believed that the penalty rules and discovery rules (which turned on the same wording) should be aligned. Accordingly, the FTT imputed into the test of carelessness a defence that amounted to having to prove the existence of a prevailing practice (which generally takes into account HMRC's views of the law). However, the FTT appears to have overlooked the fact that the prevailing practice defence in the discovery provisions is a separate rule, which operates independently of the question of carelessness. The author does not expect HMRC or the tribunal to be relying on the *Delphi* decision in this regard and the case is mentioned here for completeness.

Cases: *AB (a firm) v HMRC* (2006) Sp C 572; *Barrett v HMRC* [2015] UKFTT 329 (TC); *Supaglazing Ltd v HMRC* [2018] UKFTT 712 (TC); *Belloul v HMRC* [2020] UKFTT 312 (TC); *Loughrey v HMRC* [2021] UKFTT 252 (TC); *G C Field & Sons Ltd v HMRC* [2021] UKFTT 297 (TC); *Kingdon v HMRC* [2022] UKFTT 407 (TC); *Rizvi v HMRC* [2023] UKFTT 124 (TC); *Altunis v HMRC* [2023] UKFTT 719 (TC); *Delphi Derivatives Ltd v HMRC* [2023] UKFTT 722 (TC)

Carelessness of persons acting on the taxpayer's behalf

The *AB* approach (see **5.4.2**) was followed by the Upper Tribunal in *Sanderson* in the context of the conduct of the taxpayer's adviser. The FTT had already held that Mr Sanderson had not been negligent by reasonable reliance on his adviser, but HMRC then sought to criticise the adviser's conduct. On the facts of the case, the adviser had himself relied upon specialists, being the promoters of the scheme in which Mr Sanderson had participated. As the Upper Tribunal concluded:

> "While [the promoter] may not have been independent, [the adviser] will have been entitled to regard them as having particular expertise in relation to matters relating to the Castle Trust Scheme."

Given the meaning of the phrase "person acting on the taxpayer's behalf" (see **5.3.2** above), it will be noted that the conduct of most promoters (even if egregious) would be unlikely to justify a discovery assessment on a participant in a scheme. This was implicit from the *Kingdon* case where the taxpayers were excused from any liability for penalties when they had acted reasonably whereas their former adviser had been on a "fiscal frolic". However, the adviser's deliberate conduct would have validated the discovery assessment (had it not been set aside for other reasons).

Atherton was a tax avoidance case where it was (wrongly) believed that a tax relief could be effected through the 2007-08 tax return, even though the relief arose in the 2008-09 tax year. That belief was shared by the scheme promoters. However, the promoters did not give express guidance as to how to effect that relief and the taxpayer's accountants made a unilateral decision as to how to achieve that result. Although the promoters would probably have endorsed the approach actually taken, they were not asked to do so. The test in s. 118(5) was cited by the tribunal as meaning that the accountants had been careless.

Cases: *AB (a firm) v HMRC* (2006) Sp C 572; *Sanderson v HMRC* [2013] UKUT 623 (TCC); *Barrett v HMRC* [2015] UKFTT 329 (TC); *Atherton v HMRC* [2019] UKUT 41 (TCC); *Kingdon v HMRC* [2022] UKFTT 407 (TC)

HMRC's response

Notwithstanding this, HMRC have relentlessly pursued taxpayers with discovery assessments in cases where the taxpayers have taken professional advice (particularly in the context of marketed avoidance schemes). In doing so, they will regularly cite the few cases where they have scored a success and selectively edit certain passages from other cases in order to advance their case.

One case which illustrates the point is *Litman*. In that case, in which the taxpayers were not represented by Counsel, HMRC were able to show that the taxpayers ought to have been aware that certain transactions which formed part of the scheme had not taken place.

Consequently, it was held that the taxpayers could not reasonably have thought that their tax returns were correct when their accuracy depended on these transactions having been entered into.

The tribunal made many comments which are not considered to be controversial. For example:

> "The critical question for this Tribunal is how much enquiry should a sophisticated taxpayer be expected to make in respect of a packaged scheme in which advice has been provided by professional advisers and all documents have been drafted by them. We have concluded that the level of due diligence required of a taxpayer in respect of the technical and legal aspects of such a scheme is low, when professional advisers are involved and the relevant areas of law are technical, as is the case here. In that respect, we do not think that the Taxpayers were negligent in not understanding the details of the acquisition and disposal of the Capital Redemption Policies, the timing of the signing of the relevant documents or how the tax losses were actually being generated."

However, the tribunal continued in a way that is (it is respectfully submitted) slightly more problematic:

> "The Taxpayers argue that it was reasonable for them to rely on statements from Montpelier about how the transactions would be implemented and that no cash transfers were actually required. In this regard we would refer to the *Hanson* decision which makes it clear that a taxpayer cannot simply leave everything to his agent, it is the taxpayer's obligation to ensure that the agent has not made any errors and 'that might involve the taxpayer seeking to understand the basis upon which an entry on his return has been made by the agent'."

In particular, it is worth noting that the reference to *Hanson* omitted several key parts of what was actually said in *Hanson* (italicised below):

> "I agree with the general thrust of the guidance given in the HMRC Compliance Handbook. In particular that a taxpayer cannot simply leave everything to his agent. *A taxpayer must certainly satisfy himself that the agent has not made any obvious error.* That might involve the taxpayer seeking to understand

the basis upon which an entry on his return has been made by the agent. *However in matters that would not be straightforward to a reasonable taxpayer and where advice from an agent has been sought which is ostensibly within the agent's area of competence, the taxpayer is entitled to rely upon that advice."*

Having been instructed in two apparently very similar cases, the author is of the view that the taxpayers were particularly unlucky in *Litman*, in that the facts of the case did not necessarily justify a conclusion of carelessness. As those other cases were resolved in the taxpayers' favour without the matter being addressed by the tribunal, a clear rebuttal of the tribunal's overall approach in *Litman* was not able to be obtained. Nevertheless, a further case (*Herefordshire*) did proceed to the tribunal which concluded that the taxpayer was not careless.

In that last case, the taxpayer had taken positive steps to seek to understand the entries on the tax return and had no reason to doubt the abilities of the scheme promoters. However, the author remains of the view that that is not essential.

Furthermore, the subsequent case of *Bayliss* emphasises the need to treat the *Litman* decision with some caution. In particular, when dealing with a tax avoidance scheme (which, by its nature, is likely to deliver a tax outcome which is in comparison more favourable than the commercial outcome). In response to HMRC's allegations of negligence, the tribunal concluded:

"We also do not think that the appellant was negligent ... in failing to obtain independent financial advice. If he had that might well have reinforced the rather obvious point that the entire transaction was uncommercial (which we think was clear enough to the appellant in any event), but would not have informed the appellant about how to fill in his tax return."

Ultimately, each case should turn on its own facts. As the tribunal in *Hanson* said in its summary of the extent to which taxpayers can rely on others to defeat an allegation of carelessness:

"At the heart of this issue is the extent to which a taxpayer is required to satisfy himself that the advice he has received from a professional adviser is correct. The answer to that will depend on the particular circumstances of the case."

Cases: *Hanson v HMRC* [2012] UKFTT 314 (TC); *Litman & Newall v HMRC* [2014] UKFTT 89 (TC); *Herefordshire Property Company v HMRC* [2015] UKFTT 79 (TC); *Bayliss v HMRC* [2016] UKFTT 500 (TC)

The relevance of "white-space" disclosures

One area where great care needs to be taken is the extent to which the taxpayer has highlighted a particular issue with HMRC, either in correspondence or, more usually, in a "white-space" area of the tax return where additional disclosures may be given.

The main relevance of such disclosures in the context of discovery assessments concerns the question of insufficient disclosure (discussed in **Chapter 6**). However, some cases relating to carelessness also consider the point.

In *Rusling*, the tribunal took the view that the taxpayer had failed to take reasonable care by failing to advise HMRC of a particular series of transactions:

> "Any prudent businessman would, for his own protection, have alerted HMRC to the possibility that tax may be payable. Why would he not? If he was correct in his assumption that tax would only be paid at the end of the investment period then there was no risk in advising HMRC. If, in the alternative, that was incorrect, the fact that HMRC had been properly alerted to the possibility in his self assessment return, using the 'white space', would have been sufficient to prevent a discovery assessment being raised. We find that he was careless in not so doing."

Similarly, in *White*, the tribunal (in a case where the taxpayer was known to be confused about the correct tax treatment of a particular payment) held:

> "Applying that test, we consider that the Appellant was careless in failing to report her redundancy payment accurately on her tax return. We accept that the fact that the payment was recorded on different payslips and Forms P60 was confusing to the Appellant. We also accept that the Appellant took genuine steps to clarify the position with GMTV, ADP and ITV and that

73

> those companies failed to assist her. At that point, however, the Appellant should have sought to clarify the position with HMRC and, at least, to have noted the confusion on her tax return. We have some sympathy for the Appellant. She did make an attempt to understand the correct position and to clarify it, but having been unable to do so, in her own words she "parked it". We accept that she was under stress, stemming both from her redundancy and from her father's illness which came to light around the same time, but she was aware of the substantial amounts she had received on her redundancy and could have appended a simple statement of those amounts, and of her unsuccessful attempts to clarify the confusion over the documents she had received, in the "white space" of her tax return. Without at least such a statement, her return was inaccurate and we consider that such inaccuracy in respect of the GMTV redundancy payment was careless."

In the author's view, however, and despite these authorities, there are a number of reasons why care should be taken before assuming that a lack of disclosure automatically amounts to careless conduct so as to justify a discovery assessment:

- First, each case turns on its own merits and what is reasonable to expect of one taxpayer in one case will not necessarily be reasonable to expect of another in different circumstances.

- Secondly, the statutory test does not in fact turn on the quality of any disclosure – what HMRC need to prove is that the under-assessment was brought about by careless conduct. The under-assessment is caused by the decision to enter (or not to enter) a particular number into a particular part of the tax return – that is a process which is not impacted at all by the contents of any white-space disclosure.

In short, the author would respectfully suggest that an actual white-space disclosure highlighting an area of doubt is likely to demonstrate that the taxpayer indeed took reasonable care, but the lack of it (without anything more) should not lead to the conclusion that there has been carelessness. (Of course, a different conclusion would be reached if a taxpayer gave evidence in the white space showing a haphazard approach to his or her tax affairs.)

Example

Sienna receives income from an unusual transaction and seeks professional advice to ascertain the correct tax treatment. Her accountant in turn seeks advice from Counsel who confirms that the income is not taxable. Sienna gives full information to her accountant and the barrister so as to ensure that the advice can be safely relied upon.

Sienna accepts this advice and does not declare the income. Sienna decides not to provide details of this transaction or the fact that she has obtained advice on her tax return and, therefore, as in the cases of *Rusling* and *White*, the tax return is wholly silent on the subject.

In the author's view, if it transpires that the advice was wrong, it would be impossible to say that the under-assessment is attributable to careless conduct, either by Sienna or her accountant.

Indeed, such a view would be consistent with the Upper Tribunal's decision in *Moore*. In that case, the taxpayer sought to defeat an allegation of carelessness by relying on papers appended to his tax return which demonstrated how the taxable interest figures were calculated. (The methodology adopted was hopelessly wrong and followed advice that the taxpayer claimed to have received from an acquaintance he met at a hotel.) The tribunal held:

> "The assessments in this case – Mr Moore's self-assessments – were based not upon what he wrote on the additional sheets, but on what he entered in the boxes. In my judgment it follows, despite the initial attraction of Mr Moore's argument to which I have referred, that the tribunal's evident conclusion about what the duty of care entailed was right. His setting out the information on an additional sheet would have given Mr Moore the protection of sub-s (5), but not of sub-s (4) and, as sub-s (3) makes clear, an assessment may be made if either one of the two conditions is fulfilled."

In *Tooth*, HMRC tried to rely on this passage from *Moore* to argue that an explanation in a white space for what transpires to be an incorrect entry on the tax return cannot excuse the conduct being complained of. However, the tribunal effectively deflected the argument and focused on the relevant test as to the nature of the taxpayer's conduct. In doing so, it highlighted the fundamental difference between the cases as follows:

> "Mr Moore was relying on advice given to him in a social context ... whereas Mr Tooth had the benefit of professional advice which he acted upon inserting [what were thought to be] correct figures, albeit in the wrong box."

Cases: *Moore v HMRC* [2011] UKUT 239 (TCC); *Patsy Barber White v HMRC* [2012] UKFTT 364 (TC); *Rusling v HMRC* [2014] UKFTT 692 (TC); *Tooth v HMRC* [2016] UKFTT 723 (TC)

5.5 Deliberate conduct

5.5.1 Overview

Historically, it was rare for HMRC to seek to argue that a loss of tax was brought about deliberately (or, to use the pre-2010 wording, fraudulently). This was because the time limits that governed discovery assessments and the old penalty rules did not expressly differentiate between different types of culpable conduct.

However, the fact that different time limits now apply (see **Chapter 8** below) means that the difference can be of critical importance. Furthermore, deliberate conduct leads to more severe outcomes in the case of penalties and also brings about the risk of "naming and shaming". Consequently, this is an area which is being considered more often at the tribunal.

Law: TMA 1970, s. 29(4)

Deliberate conduct by third parties

It should be remembered that a taxpayer might be completely innocent of any wrong-doing: a discovery assessment can be made if a person acting on the taxpayer's behalf deliberately causes an under-assessment.

There is an argument that a wholly dishonest accountant (say) cannot be said to be acting on the taxpayer's behalf, because the contractual relationship between the two was based on the assumption of honest conduct. However, this argument would have to overcome the case of *Clixby* (see **5.3.2** above).

However, as shown in *Robson*, that hurdle is not insurmountable. In that case, the fraudulent adviser had not been properly authorised by the taxpayer to submit a return: indeed, the taxpayer was unaware that a return was being made, let alone knowing of its inaccurate contents.

Robson and *Clixby* both make reference to the case of *Wellington* which concerned the time when married men had to include their wives' income in their own returns. In *Wellington*, the wife had fraudulently concealed her income but, as her husband was unaware of this, there was no fraudulent conduct by "the taxpayer".

Cases: *Wellington v Reynolds (HM Inspector of Taxes)* (1962) 40 TC 209; *Clixby v Pountney (HM Inspector of Taxes)* (1967) 44 TC 515; *Robson v HMRC* [2023] UKFTT 226 (TC)

5.5.2 Causation

As with carelessness (see **5.3.1**), the statute requires the under-assessment to be attributable to the deliberate conduct. A deliberate act on its own will not be sufficient to justify a discovery assessment.

Nevertheless, especially in cases where HMRC have simply missed a time limit to assess a taxpayer on the basis of carelessness, HMRC are regularly alleging deliberate conduct in cases in which one would not normally consider there to have been any dishonesty.

For example, the author is aware of cases where HMRC have put forward the following arguments:

- the taxpayer submits a tax return and self-assessment;
- the tax return contained an error;
- the self-assessment was therefore incorrect;
- the taxpayer's submission of the tax return was a deliberate act; and
- therefore, the under-assessment was brought about by the taxpayer's deliberate act.

Generally such approaches are being rebuffed by the tribunal. See, for example, *Kinesis*, discussed further at **5.5.4** below.

Tooth (discussed more fully at **5.5.5** below) contained a most colourful rebuttal of HMRC's approach. HMRC's complaint was not simply the fact that a loss had been generated by a tax avoidance scheme but that it was a case in which the loss had been carried back to the previous tax year. Furthermore (and presumably this was the most egregious part of the case from HMRC's perspective), in accordance with the advice received (which had been endorsed by leading Counsel but which has since proven to be incorrect), the loss was "utilised" by reducing the self-assessment calculation for that earlier year. In order to effect this reduction, the loss had to be put in a box which, according to the rubric on the tax return, was clearly unsuitable for the purpose. HMRC described this as "forcing" the loss onto the earlier year's return. They argued that to use the partnership pages of a return to record an employment loss was *prima facie* deliberate conduct for the purposes of the discovery assessment rules. The tribunal disagreed:

> "The deliberate (or indeed careless) conduct necessary to enable the issue of a discovery assessment and extend the time limits for doing so must involve more than the completion of a tax return which, in itself, is a deliberate act. As a person completing a return must do so intentionally or knowingly, and can hardly do so accidentally, HMRC's argument effectively eliminates any distinction between "careless" and "deliberate" rendering otiose the necessity for the different conduct related time limits in s 36 TMA. [Counsel for HMRC's] attempt to argue otherwise, saying that if the wrong figures were entered in the right boxes it might be careless but if the right figures were entered in the wrong boxes it would be deliberate, was somewhat reminiscent of, and about as convincing as, Eric Morecambe's riposte to Andre Previn about 'playing all the notes, but not necessarily in the right order'."

The next paragraph of the decision stated the correct proposition:

> "... a causal link between the insufficiency of tax and the deliberate action is required and it is necessary to ask what a taxpayer has done, deliberately, to bring about that insufficiency. In this case the question is what did Mr Tooth do, intending or knowing it would bring about an insufficiency of tax?"

Nevertheless, there are bound to be many cases where taxpayers do not have the resolve or confidence to fight HMRC (or where they prefer to remain outside the public gaze) and, therefore, the spurious allegations are going unchecked.

In *Baloch*, the tribunal rejected HMRC's argument that failure to check a tax return amounts to deliberate behaviour (but accepted that it could well indicate carelessness). Nevertheless, it upheld the assessments in that case simply because it did not believe that the taxpayer ("an intelligent, professional person") would not have taken more steps to check that what he was doing was correct.

Furthermore, in *Delphi*, a case being argued by experienced Counsel on both sides, the FTT took the view (in the context of the similarly worded rule concerning careless conduct) that there was no need for any causal link. As discussed at **5.4.3**, that decision should be treated with some considerable caution. Indeed, the decision does not even suggest that the FTT's view of the law was actually put forward or argued by either party.

Law: TMA 1970, s. 29(4)

Cases: *Kinesis Positive Recruitment Ltd v HMRC* [2016] UKFTT 178 (TC); *Tooth v HMRC* [2016] UKFTT 723 (TC); *Baloch v HMRC* [2017] UKFTT 665 (TC); *Delphi Derivatives Ltd v HMRC* [2023] UKFTT 722 (TC)

5.5.3   Meaning of "deliberate"

The meaning of "deliberate" is not without its own controversies.

The starting point for a tribunal is to apply the normal meaning of the words when deciding whether a situation has been "brought about … deliberately by the taxpayer or a person acting on his behalf".

A partial statutory definition

The statute makes a very subtle extension to this by providing that it will also catch cases where:

> "a loss of tax or a situation … arises as a result of a deliberate inaccuracy in a document given to [HMRC] by or on behalf of that person."

As the Supreme Court held in *Tooth*, this provision ensures that the statutory test is met as long as the conduct which brings about or "results in" an insufficiency consists of an inaccuracy in a document given to HMRC. It is not necessary for the insufficiency to be deliberate, as long as the inaccuracy itself is. As the court summarised:

> "it decouples the insufficiency from the requisite intention, provided that the deliberate inaccuracy causes it [i.e. the insufficiency] in fact."

Furthermore, as the court continued, it paves the way to conduct being held to be "deliberate", so as to justify a discovery assessment, without necessarily being fraudulent.

Law: TMA 1970, s. 118(7)
Case: *HMRC v Tooth* [2021] UKSC 17

HMRC's definition

HMRC's manuals give the following meaning of deliberate:

> "A deliberate ... inaccuracy occurs when a person gives HMRC a document that they know contains an inaccuracy. It is not necessary to demonstrate that the person knew what the accurate figure was, only that they knew the figure they put on the document was not accurate."

It is clear, therefore, that HMRC consider "deliberate" conduct to involve *knowledge* that the document was wrong – this is more than simple recklessness.

Guidance: CH 81150

5.5.4   The evolving case law up to 2020

There have been generally two strands of authorities developing in respect of the test of "deliberate conduct". One requires actual knowledge of the underlying inaccuracy, whereas the second strand is broader and incorporates a reckless disregard of the truth.

The Supreme Court's decision in *Tooth* (discussed at **5.5.5**) does not fully resolve this debate.

Case: *HMRC v Tooth* [2021] UKSC 17

The narrower approach

In *Contractors*, the tribunal gave the following guidance on the meaning of "deliberate":

"the term 'deliberate' should be interpreted as being an action taken consciously where there was an appreciation that there was a choice."

In *Kinesis*, the tribunal considered that to be "a useful starting point" but also referred to the OED definition which included the phrase "with full intention".

In that case, the tribunal had to choose between a number of different possible meanings of deliberate for the purposes of the legislation. It immediately rejected the notion (which was tantamount to creating strict liability) that there would be deliberate conduct if an action took place which should not have happened.

That was a case concerning whether or not a VAT invoice had been deliberately issued by an unauthorised person. The tribunal concluded that such an action fell within the statutory test if:

- the company deliberately issued an invoice purporting to be a VAT invoice; and

- at the time, the company knew it was not an authorised person.

Besides those two conditions, the tribunal considered that no specific knowledge of wrongdoing was necessary.

Although those two cases provide some guidance, they are of limited relevance when it comes to discovery assessments, where the statutory test is different. In short, especially given the fact that deliberate conduct is the more serious sibling of carelessness, the author is of the view that the statute requires there to be a dishonest intent (or something very close to it). For example, in *Auxilium*, the tribunal endorsed HMRC's own guidance (cited above), continuing as follows:

"In our view, a deliberate inaccuracy occurs when a taxpayer knowingly provides HMRC with a document that contains an error with the intention that HMRC should rely upon it as an accurate document. This is a subjective test. The question is not whether a reasonable taxpayer might have made the same error or even whether this taxpayer failed to take all reasonable steps to ensure that the return was accurate. It is a question of the knowledge and intention of the particular taxpayer at the time."

In *Scott*, HMRC argued that the taxpayers' conduct must have been deliberate because "based on the significant difference between the income returned and that which has now been assessed they argue that Mrs Scott must have known that there was missing income". The tribunal, however, considered this to be insufficient:

> "Again we find ourselves faced with uncertainty. Our overall impression was that Mr and Mrs Scott had a somewhat disorganised approach to their personal finances, as witnessed by the complete lack of underlying records as regards cash receipts and banking. We therefore consider it quite possible that any underdeclaration was caused by carelessness rather than by deliberate default. Using the same logic for the uncertainty surrounding this issue as we did for the uncertainty surrounding the tax assessments we therefore find that HMRC have failed to discharge the burden of proof on them to demonstrate that there was a deliberate under-declaration of income by Mrs Scott."

In *Tooth*, the taxpayer was acting in accordance with professional advice and neither he nor his advisers knew that the approach he was taken would prove to be incorrect. As the FTT made clear, this fact was sufficient to disprove any allegations that Mr Tooth "knew" or "intended" to bring about an insufficiency of tax:

> "It therefore follows that there was nothing that Mr Tooth, or a person acting on his behalf, did that deliberately brought about an insufficiency of tax."

Cases: *Contractors 4 U Ltd v HMRC* [2016] UKFTT 17 (TC); *Kinesis Positive Recruitment Ltd v HMRC* [2016] UKFTT 178 (TC); *Auxilium Project Management Ltd v HMRC* [2016] UKFTT 249 (TC); *Scott v HMRC* [2016] UKFTT 599 (TC); *Tooth v HMRC* [2016] UKFTT 723 (TC)

The broader approach

The alternative strand is demonstrated in the case of *Clynes*. There, the tribunal considered that deliberate conduct might be capable of being shown "where it is found that the person consciously or intentionally chose not to find out the correct position, in particular, where the circumstances are such that the person knew that he should do so." This broader definition had been repeatedly rejected by subsequent tribunal decisions. However, it regularly features in HMRC's arguments as if it were the only judicial statement on the subject.

Such repetition has borne fruit because, in *Chohan*, the tribunal held (repeating the wording used in *Cavendish*, a case which shared the same judge):

> "It is dishonest for a person deliberately to shut their eyes to facts which they would prefer not to know. If he or she does so, they are taken to have actual knowledge of the facts to which they shut their eyes."

As the tribunal continued: " 'Blind-eye' knowledge approximates to knowledge." The question which was not addressed, however, is whether "approximation" is enough.

Similarly, in *Cation* and in reliance on *Clynes*, the tribunal held that the taxpayer's apparent shrewdness and business acumen was sufficient to persuade it that an error in the tax return was unlikely to be careless and therefore was deliberate.

A less controversial variation of the *Clynes* theme found support in *Farrow*: proceeding on a basis that was "so uncommercial and too good to be true that the [taxpayer] should have realised that they could not possibly serve any legitimate purpose". Earlier in the decision, this additional variation was described as not having "any real belief [in the position shown on the return]".

Similarly, in *CPR*, the Upper Tribunal made the following observations:

> "where a taxpayer suspects that a document contained an inaccuracy but deliberately and without good reason chooses not to confirm the true position before submitting the document to HMRC then the inaccuracy is deliberate on the part of the taxpayer. If it were otherwise then a person who believed there was a high probability that their return contained errors but chose not to investigate would never be

subject to a deliberate penalty. However, the suspicion must be more than merely fanciful."

Cases: *Clynes v HMRC* [2016] UKFTT 369 (TC); *Farrow v HMRC* [2019] UKFTT 200 (TC); *Cavendish Ships Stores Ltd v HMRC* [2021] UKFTT 257 (TC); *Chohan Management Ltd v HMRC* [2021] UKFTT 196 (TC); *Cation v HMRC* [2021] UKFTT 311 (TC); *CPR Commercials Ltd v HMRC* [2023] UKUT 61 (TCC)

5.5.5   *The Tooth decision*

The Supreme Court's decision in *Tooth* should provide a clear starting point for any future discussions of the deliberate test, although some of the earlier case law might still need to be considered in particular cases. Indeed, the facts of *Tooth* are quite unusual and the Supreme Court's deliberations must be seen in the light of what had happened in that case.

In *Tooth*, the taxpayer believed that the *pro forma* tax return was deficient and wrongly failed to allow him to obtain a particular kind of relief. Accordingly, through his advisers, he effected a work-around by using a different box on the return to achieve his goal, but then explained his actions in a white-space entry.

The Supreme Court made the following observations:

> "Suppose for example that Mr Tooth had entered the employment-related loss in the partnership box without providing any explanation of its true source and nature, intending the Revenue to believe that it derived from a partnership business and occurred during the 2007-8 tax year. It would still have generated a negative tax liability for 2007-8 in the amount which he genuinely believed to be true. But if that negative amount (and the consequent insufficiency) was the result of entering the loss in the partnership box, as a partnership loss, (rather than elsewhere in the return) then we consider that the deliberate limb of the first condition in section 29(4) would have been fulfilled. Such a presentation in his return would have misled the Revenue from having a full understanding of the information relevant to assessing his self-assessment."

What is key here is the assumed motive of the taxpayer "intending the Revenue to believe that [the loss] derived from a partnership business and occurred during the 2007-8 tax year" (i.e. intending HMRC to draw the natural inferences from the actual boxes used by the taxpayer).

HMRC sought to argue that any inaccurate statement would be sufficient to meet the statutory test, provided that the statement was deliberately made (even in cases where the person making the statement believed the statement to be true). In other words, as long as the inaccurate statement was not made carelessly or unintentionally, HMRC could justify a discovery assessment. However, the Supreme Court rejected this approach and emphatically ruled that there must be "a statement which, when made, was deliberately inaccurate".

In summary, their Lordships concluded:

> "there will have to be demonstrated an intention to mislead the Revenue on the part of the taxpayer as to the truth of the relevant statement".

The court left to be decided in another case whether it would be sufficient for HMRC, instead of proving an intention to mislead, to prove recklessness as to whether the statement would mislead HMRC.

In *Rodriguez-Issa*, albeit without reference to the *Tooth* decision, the FTT expressed the following view concerning this point:

> "We agree that an inaccuracy may be held to be deliberate where it is found that the person consciously or intentionally chose not to find out the correct position. However, as the Tribunal indicated in *Clynes*, this will be a question of fact and degree that must be determined on a case by case basis. Care must be taken not to blur the line between careless and deliberate conduct."

The final limb of the court's analysis in *Tooth* concerned the question of what amounted to an inaccuracy: was it sufficient for HMRC to show an individual entry to have been made deliberately wrongly or should entries be considered in their full context? This was relevant because Mr Tooth used boxes on the tax return to enter figures that were clearly not destined for those boxes, but then sought to explain those entries elsewhere on the return. The court made it clear that the correct approach is "rather than concluding that there is an inaccuracy by applying tunnel-vision to a particular part of the document, and ignoring the rest, the true meaning of that part is ascertained from a reading of the document as a whole".

Cases: *HMRC v Tooth* [2021] UKSC 17; *Rodriguez-Issa v HMRC* [2021] UKFTT 154 (TC)

5.5.6   Cases after Tooth

Generally, it seems that the tribunal is not rejecting the *Clynes* approach out of hand, but is limiting it to extreme cases of recklessness. For example, in *Quinns*, the FTT made the following observation:

> "We can see how there may be circumstances where a taxpayer has deliberately put his or her head in the sand and thus deliberately chosen to maintain a state of ignorance in order to disavow responsibility for an inaccuracy. However, in order for that to be the case, we think that the taxpayer must at least suspect that an entry in the tax return is inaccurate and then make a conscious decision not to explore whether or not that is the case."

Similarly, in *Arthur*, having first endorsed the *Auxilium* decision (see **5.5.4**), the FTT proceeded to approve the *Clynes* approach by saying:

> "if a taxpayer is aware of the existence of facts or circumstances which they know will or might render a return inaccurate and they choose not to investigate further in the light of those facts or circumstances in order to verify the accuracy of the return, then any inaccuracy which they would have uncovered if they had done so should be regarded as being a deliberate inaccuracy so far as the taxpayer is concerned."

The *Arthur* case concerned assessments made against a husband and wife in the light of the husband's earlier conviction for cheating the public revenue. The FTT held, in the absence of any evidence of earlier knowledge, that the wife's conduct could be described as deliberate only once HMRC's criminal investigation into her husband became public knowledge (being the date on which a raid took place).

In *Kingdon*, the FTT held that an adviser allocating figures between a partnership and a company as he saw fit – and without any analysis of the underlying commercial activities of the respective trading entities – amounted to deliberate conduct.

Cases: *Auxilium Project Management Ltd v HMRC* [2016] UKFTT 249 (TC); *JT Quinns Ltd v HMRC* [2021] UKFTT 454 (TC); *Arthur v HMRC* [2022] UKFTT 216 (TC); *Kingdon v HMRC* [2022] UKFTT 407 (TC)

5.6   Other taxes

5.6.1   Corporation tax

The corporation tax legislation does not provide any statutory pointers as to the meaning of when a loss of tax is brought about carelessly or deliberately. However, the qualifications in TMA 1970, s. 118 are incorporated into the corporation tax code by FA 1998, s. 117(2).

Law: FA 1998, s. 117(2)

Actions by third parties

In the case of companies, the statute provides for three categories of person whose careless or deliberate conduct can justify a discovery assessment.

In addition to the company itself and any person acting on the company's behalf, the statute brings in "a person who was a partner of the company at the relevant time".

The "relevant time" is not defined but is assumed to mean the time when the culpable conduct occurred.

Law: FA 1998, Sch. 18, para. 43

5.6.2   SDLT

The statutory extensions of the meaning of "careless" and "deliberate" are found in FA 2003, Sch. 10, para. 31A.

Law: FA 2003, Sch. 10, para. 30(2), 31A

Actions by third parties

As with corporation tax, the SDLT statute provides for a third category of person whose careless or deliberate conduct can justify a discovery assessment.

In addition to the purchaser and any person acting on the purchaser's behalf, the statute brings in "a person who was a partner of the purchaser at the relevant time".

The "relevant time" is not defined but is assumed to mean the time when the culpable conduct occurred.

Law: FA 2003, Sch. 10, para. 30(2)

5.6.3   ATED

The statutory extensions of the meaning of careless and deliberate are found in FA 2013, Sch. 33, para. 26.

Law: FA 2013, Sch. 33, para. 24(2), 26

Actions by third parties

As with corporation tax and SDLT, the ATED statute provides for a third category of person whose careless or deliberate conduct can justify a discovery assessment.

In addition to the taxpayer and any person acting on the taxpayer's behalf, the statute brings in "a person who was a partner of the taxpayer at the relevant time".

The "relevant time" is not defined (for these purposes, although it is defined for the purposes of para. 24(3)) but is assumed to mean the time when the culpable conduct occurred.

Law: FA 2013, Sch. 33, para. 24(2)

5.6.4   Digital services tax

In the case of the digital services tax, the rules are the same as for income tax.

Law: FA 2020, Sch. 8, para. 20(2)

5.6.5   Public interest business protection tax

In the case of the public interest business protection tax, the rules are the same as for income tax.

Law: FA 2022, Sch. 10, para. 18(3)

5.6.6   Multinational top-up tax

In the case of multinational top-up tax, the careless or deliberate conduct of a group member (or a person acting on behalf of the group) can justify a discovery assessment.

Law: F(No. 2)A 2023, Sch. 14, para. 28(3)

5.7   Other discovery provisions

5.7.1   Non-resident capital gains tax

The equivalent provisions

Although the provisions do not apply to tax years after 2018-19, the potential for a discovery assessment in respect of an earlier period remains.

The equivalent provisions are found in TMA 1970, s. 29A(4). There is no practical difference between the non-resident CGT rules and those otherwise applying for income tax and CGT.

Law: TMA 1970, s. 29A(4)

5.7.2   Partnership returns

The equivalent provisions

The equivalent provisions are found in TMA 1970, s. 30B(5). There is no practical difference between the rules for partnerships and those otherwise applying for income tax and CGT.

Law: TMA 1970, s. 30B(5)

6.   Insufficiency of disclosure

6.1   Introduction

As noted in **Chapter 4**, two additional conditions apply in cases where a taxpayer has submitted a return for the relevant period. HMRC need to show that at least one of those conditions is satisfied.

This Chapter considers the second of those two conditions. The alternative condition is discussed in **Chapter 5**.

As was noted at **2.1.2** above, the purpose of the restrictions on HMRC's right to make a discovery assessment was to afford taxpayers a greater sense of finality in the self-assessment era.

The *quid pro quo* chosen by Parliament was (to paraphrase the legislation and excluding cases involving carelessness or deliberate conduct) to preclude discovery assessments in those cases where HMRC ought to have been able to rectify the situation through the means of a self-assessment enquiry.

However, the precise test laid down by Parliament has led to considerable uncertainty and litigation.

Law: TMA 1970, s. 29(3)

6.2   The statutory test

6.2.1   Overview

The statutory test poses the question: would an HMRC officer be aware of the situation (i.e. the perceived under-assessment) on the basis of information made available to him or her.

The question is posed at the last opportunity HMRC would have to address this perceived under-assessment via an enquiry.

If an officer would have been so aware, then HMRC may not make a discovery assessment. In other words, if HMRC are to rely on this condition, they need to show that an HMRC officer could not have been aware of the under-assessment on the basis of information made available to HMRC.

6.2.2 Four elements

The statutory test reads as follows:

"… at the time when an officer of the Board–

(a) ceased to be entitled to give notice of his intention to enquire into the taxpayer's return under section 8 or 8A of this Act in respect of the relevant year of assessment; or

(b) in a case where a notice of enquiry into the return was given–

    (i) issued a partial closure notice as regards a matter to which the situation mentioned in subsection (1) above relates, or

    (ii) if no such partial closure notice was issued, issued a final closure notice,

the officer could not have been reasonably expected, on the basis of the information made available to him before that time, to be aware of the situation mentioned in subsection (1) above."

There are therefore four elements to the statutory test:

- first, identifying the officer (see **6.3** below);
- secondly, the time at which the officer's knowledge is tested (see **6.4** below);
- thirdly, the information made available to the officer for these purposes (see **6.5** below); and
- fourthly, the level of awareness needed (see **6.6** below).

Law: TMA 1970, s. 29(5)

6.3 The officer

Most case law refers to the officer as the "hypothetical officer". However, the statute gives no clue as to who this officer is and what skills (if any) should be attributed to that individual.

The question was not generally relevant in the earlier cases which made reference variously to:

- "the general knowledge and skill that might reasonably be attributed to an officer";
- "equipped with a reasonable knowledge of tax law";
- "the general knowledge and skill that might reasonably be attributed to him"; and
- "an ordinary competent inspector".

The matter was of particular relevance, however, in the case of *Charlton* which (as well as considering these earlier definitions) concluded as follows:

"Our conclusion on this point, therefore, is that s 29(5) does not require the hypothetical officer to be given the characteristics of an officer of general competence, knowledge or skill only. The officer must be assumed to have such level of knowledge and understanding that would reasonably be expected in an officer considering the particular information provided by the taxpayer."

In short, if the relevant information (see **6.5** below) before the officer shows that the taxpayer has received (say) a life assurance gain, the officer is deemed to have sufficient knowledge to understand the taxation of life assurance gains, at least so far as is relevant to what has been disclosed.

Conversely, if the relevant information gives no indication as to the types of transaction in which the taxpayer has been involved, the level of skill and knowledge attributed to the hypothetical officer is accordingly reduced.

In *Beagles*, the Upper Tribunal gave the following guidance as to the hypothetical officer (based on the facts of that case where the relevant material before the officer referred to relevant discounted securities):

"The hypothetical officer is an officer of general competence, knowledge or skill with a reasonable knowledge and understanding of the law. In our view, that would encompass a knowledge of the legislation relating to relevant discounted securities ... and even if he or she did not, we would expect the officer to acquire that knowledge, given that the officer is directed to the legislation by the appendix to the return."

We would expect the hypothetical officer to be reasonably acquainted with the status of the case law on the *Ramsay* approach and to be aware for example of the House of Lords decision in *MacNiven v Westmoreland Investments Limited* [2001] STC 237, [2001] BTC 44 ("*MacNiven*"), the leading case at the time. We would also expect the officer to have a reasonable degree of commercial awareness (and, for example, to be aware, in broad terms, of the commercial level of interest rates at the time).

... the test does assume that the hypothetical officer will apply the appropriate level of knowledge and skill to the information that is treated as being available before the level of awareness is tested."

It will be seen that the officer's knowledge will be time-specific (although it is thought that an officer should not be incapable of predicting certain likely refinements of the case law).

This broad approach has been generally accepted, although an alternative view was mooted in the Scottish case of *Pattullo*. There, the Upper Tribunal considered the approach taken in *Charlton* as "complex, sophisticated and nuanced" (doubting that such an approach had been intended by Parliament) but went along with it as a result of the body of case law that has evolved since *Charlton*. It is the *Charlton* approach that has so far prevailed.

Cases: *HMRC v Charlton (and others)* [2012] UKUT 770 (TCC); *Beagles v HMRC* [2018] UKUT 380 (TCC); *Pattullo v HMRC* [2016] UKUT 270 (TCC)

6.4   The timing

The officer's knowledge is fixed at a single point in time:

- If there had been no enquiry into the taxpayer's relevant return, then that point in time is the last moment at which HMRC could have validly opened a statutory enquiry into the return.
- If an enquiry had been opened into the taxpayer's relevant return, the point in time depends on whether a final or partial closure notice is given:
  - If a partial closure notice has been given in respect of the matter covered by the supposed loss of tax, the

> > point in time is when that partial closure notice is given.
>
> - o Otherwise, the point in time is when a final closure notice is given.

A literal application of the statutory words can give rise to potential difficulties.

Example

Ronald submits his 2022-23 tax return on 25 January 2024. He has inadvertently (but, assume neither carelessly nor deliberately) omitted income of £10,000 and, therefore, he under-assesses himself.

Realising the error when preparing his 2023-25 tax return, Ronald promptly writes to his tax office, which receives the letter on 25 January 2025 (which happens to be the last date for opening an enquiry into the 2022-23 tax return, had HMRC been so minded). The letter fully explains the omission.

As the hypothetical officer *could*, on the basis of the information made available to him at the time at which the enquiry window closed, have been aware of the under-assessment, it is arguable that the test in s. 29(5) is *not* met and so no discovery assessment can be made.

The author considers, however, that the courts would interpret the provision slightly more sensibly so as to accord with the statutory purpose – especially as the word "reasonably" appears elsewhere in the subsection. On this basis, it is considered that a discovery assessment can be avoided only if *reasonable* notice were given (say, Ronald in the above example had written to HMRC a full month before the enquiry window closes). The fact that HMRC might not get round to actioning post that quickly is of little relevance. Indeed, as was noted in *Veltema* itself, how HMRC actually conduct themselves (or are supposed to conduct themselves) "cannot, of course, be an aid to construction of TMA 1970".

It should be noted, however, that such a "sensible" interpretation risks leading to uncertainties and inconsistent treatment between different cases. To date, it is not thought that the tribunals have had to grapple with this question.

Case: *Langham (HM Inspector of Taxes) v Veltema* [2004] EWCA Civ 193

6.5   Information made available to the officer

6.5.1   Overview

Contrary to what was originally thought to be the case, the statute is prescriptive and provides an exhaustive list of information that is deemed to be before the hypothetical officer for these purposes (see **6.5.3** below).

If a document falls outside that list then, no matter how unlikely it would be that any real-life officer would disregard its contents, the information on that document cannot be attributed to the hypothetical officer.

6.5.2   Langham v Veltema

The earliest key case on these rules is *Langham v Veltema*. Until the Court of Appeal gave its decision in that case, it was widely thought that the hypothetical officer could be expected to undertake a series of checks (behind the equally hypothetical scenes) to verify the correctness of the taxpayer's return. In addition to this series of checks, the officer would have imputed to him or her certain information by virtue of a deeming provision in s. 29(6).

According to the Court of Appeal, however, the list of information in s. 29(6) is in fact the full list of information deemed to be before the hypothetical officer. In other words, the hypothetical officer is neither expected nor required to embark upon any form of investigation, besides reviewing the information which the statute has deemed to place before him. As Auld LJ held:

> "it is plain from the wording of the statutory test in s. 29(5) that it is concerned, not with what an inspector could reasonably have been expected to do, but with what he could have been reasonably expected to be aware of. It speaks of an inspector's objective awareness, from the information made available to him by the taxpayer, of 'the situation' mentioned in s. 29(1), namely an actual insufficiency in the assessment, not an objective awareness that he should do something to check whether there is such an insufficiency, as suggested by Park J. If he is uneasy about the sufficiency of the assessment, he can exercise his power of enquiry under s. 9A and is given plenty of

95

time in which to complete it before the discovery provisions of s. 29 take effect."

It is the author's view that the judge's phrase "an actual insufficiency" should not be given too much weight as it does not reflect the statutory words. Indeed, taken literally, it can give rise to errors in the "awareness" test discussed at **6.6** below. See, in particular, the discussion below on *Corbally-Stourton*.

This was expressly stated to be the law in *Beagles*:

"The test does not require that the actual insufficiency is identified on the face of the return."

Cases: *Langham (HM Inspector of Taxes) v Veltema* [2004] EWCA Civ 193; *Beagles v HMRC* [2018] UKUT 380 (TCC)

6.5.3   The list of information deemed to be before the officer

Overview

Section 29(6) provides for five categories of information (to be increased to six after the introduction of MTD) that may be deemed to be before the hypothetical officer. The first three (or four once MTD is in force) contain information that will actually have been made available to HMRC, whereas the last two deem the hypothetical officer to have other information which might or might not have been previously disclosed to HMRC.

The logic of the last two categories is to reflect the real-world situation where an actual officer (based upon information already in his or her possession) would (or should) request additional documentation from the taxpayer (or, potentially, a third party) and, in the real world, would have at least a year in order to open an enquiry to facilitate such a request.

Actual information previously disclosed to HMRC

The first three categories of information deemed to be before the hypothetical officer are:

- anything contained in the taxpayer's tax return for the relevant tax year or in any document accompanying the return;

- anything contained in a claim made by the taxpayer (acting in the same capacity as that in which he made the tax return) for the relevant tax year or in any document accompanying any such claim; and

- in cases where an enquiry has been opened into the return or claim, anything contained in any document (or accounts or particulars) produced or furnished by the taxpayer to HMRC for the purposes of the enquiry.

In *Buckingham*, the tribunal confirmed that the references to "enquiry" relate to formal enquiries (e.g. under TMA, s. 9A) rather than non-statutory investigations. In that case, a s. 9A enquiry had been invalidly opened; when this was realised, the subsequent "closure notice" was replaced by a discovery assessment. The tribunal held that information provided by the taxpayer in the course of the invalid enquiry could not be imputed to the hypothetical officer.

From 6 April 2024, the original commencement date for Making Tax Digital, an additional category will be added:

- anything contained in the taxpayer's periodic updates.

It should be noted that s. 29(7)(a) then expands upon certain phrases so that the list is effectively expanded to include the following as well:

- anything contained in the taxpayer's tax return for either of the two previous tax years or in any document accompanying those returns;

- (from 6 April 2015, but relevant only for disposals up to 5 April 2019) anything contained in a non-resident CGT tax return by the taxpayer which contains an advance self-assessment relating to the tax year or either of the two previous tax years or in any document accompanying such a return; and

- if the taxpayer is an individual (and so the return is under TMA 1970, s. 8) and the taxpayer carries on a trade, profession or business in partnership, anything in the partnership's own tax return either for the relevant tax year or for either of the two previous tax years.

These expansions are not modified so as to include materials included in MTD periodic returns.

Furthermore, s. 29(7)(b) expands the meaning of "taxpayer" to include a person acting on the taxpayer's behalf (see also **5.3.2**). This therefore means that information provided to HMRC by a taxpayer's adviser in the course of an enquiry (say) will be deemed to be before the hypothetical officer. Of course, the provision does not mean that the contents of the adviser's own tax return (say) is imputed to the hypothetical officer.

More importantly, information actually provided to HMRC by third parties will generally be excluded from being before the hypothetical officer, unless the third party is acting on the taxpayer's behalf. But there can be situations where third party information provided to HMRC will be imputed to the hypothetical officer.

Law: TMA 1970, s. 29(6)(a)-(c), (7); SI 2021/1079, reg. 2
Case: *Buckingham v HMRC* [2023] UKFTT 358 (TC)

Information deemed to be available

The final two categories allow additional information to be deemed to be before the hypothetical officer. In both cases, the officer has to be deemed to be aware of both the *existence* of the information and its *relevance* to the potential under-assessment.

This can arise in two situations:

- first, if the hypothetical officer can reasonably be expected to infer the existence and relevance from any other documentation deemed to be before him or her (under the rules discussed above); or
- alternatively, if HMRC are actually notified of these facts in writing by either the taxpayer or a person acting on the taxpayer's behalf.

Unlike the list of information actually made available to HMRC, these categories can allow taxpayers to rely on information not in HMRC's possession (although the categories also allow certain information held elsewhere within HMRC to be deemed to be before the hypothetical officer).

Another difference in relation to these two categories is that the statute does not require the information to be contained in any specific form or document: it simply has to exist and be relevant (or, more strictly, HMRC have to have been notified of its existence and relevance or reasonably be expected to infer it from other information).

Law: TMA 1970, s. 29(6)(d), (7)

6.5.4   Practical application of these rules

As the legislation is prescriptively drafted, information that does not readily fall under any of these headings cannot be imputed to the hypothetical officer, however unrealistic this restriction might be. This can be best illustrated with an example.

Example

Frederick is an employee, whose employer provides a car benefit, the details of which are provided each year on a form P11D. Frederick omits the details of his car benefit from his tax return.

The mere fact that Frederick is an employee does not tell the hypothetical officer that there is reason to believe a P11D is in existence, let alone that Frederick might have received a car benefit.

Even if Frederick had noted the existence of a P11D (for example, by noting in the white space that he had received travel expenses of £124 "per P11D"), complete silence as to the possibility of a car benefit will mean that the hypothetical officer is not deemed to know that a car benefit had been received.

This is the case even though any real officer (or any computerised equivalent) would undoubtedly have cross-checked the employer's P11D return with the contents of Frederick's tax return.

The only way Frederick can put the fact of the car benefit before the hypothetical officer is by making a disclosure of the fact that he has a company car and/or that he has not included all of the figures from his P11D.

On the other hand, there have been cases in which information has been deemed to be before the hypothetical officer.

For example, in *Blum*, the tribunal accepted that a P14 (which can be expected to be given to any employee with reported employment income) was before the hypothetical officer. Rather inexplicably, however, the tribunal followed the wording of *Langham v Veltema* a bit too literally and concluded that the mismatch between the P14 figure and the return employment income was not sufficient to alert the hypothetical officer to the possible under-assessment.

Similarly, in *Loughrey*, information from HMRC's Real Time Information (a system by which PAYE records are maintained in real time) was held to be information that can be imputed to a hypothetical officer in a case where the tax return made it clear that the taxpayer was an employee.

Furthermore, in *While*, it was acknowledged that information held by an actual officer in the course of an enquiry could not be imputed to the hypothetical officer. Nor could it be deemed to be before the hypothetical officer even though the actual officer had made express reference to it in her written notes of the meeting which were sent *to* the taxpayer. This is because s. 29(6) is limited to information provided to HMRC *by* the taxpayer (or a person acting on the taxpayer's behalf). However, because the meeting notes were subsequently acknowledged by the taxpayer's accountant in a response to the officer, the hypothetical officer was then deemed to have seen them.

In *McCumiskey*, the tribunal (in the context of a tax return fraudulently submitted without the taxpayer's knowledge or consent) considered that a return whose entries were so obviously wrong was in itself sufficient to put the hypothetical officer on notice of an under-assessment. The author considers that this part of the tribunal's decision stretches the statutory test as far as it can possibly go in favour of a taxpayer: it is unclear whether it would be followed as readily in a case where there would be less obvious sympathy towards the taxpayer.

In *Charlton*, the Upper Tribunal considered that the details of a DOTAS disclosure (form "AAG1", made by a scheme promoter) should be imputed to the hypothetical officer by virtue of the fact that the taxpayer's return contained a scheme reference number. In such a case, the hypothetical officer could easily have inferred the existence of such a disclosure explaining the workings of the arrangements (as the scheme reference number could not have been generated without one) – similarly, the relevance to the potential under-assessment should have been easily inferred.

In *Sheth*, HMRC accepted that a further DOTAS form, AAG4, should similarly be imputed to the hypothetical officer.

In the above six cases, the hypothetical officer was deemed to possess information that was actually held elsewhere within HMRC. However, that is not a requirement under the rules. Indeed, a potentially more useful application of the rules is to deem the hypothetical officer to have information that is not actually in HMRC's possession. Typically, this will arise in cases where a detailed document, for example a valuation report, has been obtained (and used to produce the figures on the tax return) but is not provided to HMRC. Following the *Langham v Veltema* decision, HMRC published the following guidance:

> "Most taxpayers who state that a valuation has been used, by whom it has been carried out, and that it was carried out by a named independent and suitably qualified valuer if that was the case, on the appropriate basis, will be able, for all practical purposes, to rely on protection from a later discovery assessment, provided those statements are true."

It should be noted that the guidance is poorly written and (strictly construed) not relevant in most cases where it might otherwise be useful (indeed, it could not be relied upon by someone in Mr Veltema's position because of the restrictions in cases involving connected parties). In short, it is better to err on the side of caution and provide more information rather than less. Nevertheless, HMRC take the view:

> "Information will not be treated as being made available where the total amount supplied is so extensive that an officer 'could not have been reasonably expected to be aware' of the significance of particular information and the officer's attention has not been drawn to it by the taxpayer or taxpayer's representative."

This point is, as yet, untested in the tribunals. However, in a very different context in *Clipper*, the tribunal did consider that a taxpayer had not received a notice from HMRC when it was included in a bundle of documents for a particular hearing but the notice was not germane to that hearing nor brought to the taxpayer's attention.

See also **Appendix 2**.

Cases: *Blum v HMRC* [2018] UKFTT 152 (TC); *While v HMRC* [2012] UKFTT 58 (TC); *HMRC v Charlton (and others)* [2012] UKUT 770 (TCC); *Clipper Group Holdings Ltd v HMRC* [2016] UKFTT 712 (TC); *Loughrey v HMRC* [2021] UKFTT 252 (TC); *McCumiskey v HMRC* [2022] UKFTT 128 (TC); *Sheth v HMRC* [2023] UKFTT 368 (TC)

Guidance: *Statement of Practice* 01/2006

6.6 Awareness

The next issue to be considered is whether, armed with the relevant information, the hypothetical officer could reasonably be expected to be aware of the suspected insufficiency. In other words, has enough information been disclosed to HMRC (or deemed to be before them)?

In *Sheth*, the tribunal observed:

> "It is also clear from *Hicks* that the adequacy or otherwise of the disclosure depends on the complexity of the arrangements under consideration. And this complexity can be complexity of fact and/or law. Whilst the adequacy of the disclosure will determine whether the hypothetical officer was made aware of the actual insufficiency, it is likely that in less complex cases, the disclosure needed to generate that awareness will be less detailed than in more complex cases. This seems largely common sense to us."

However, that still leaves open the question as to what is meant by "aware".

It is the author's firm view that awareness equates to the same level of knowledge as would justify an officer making an assessment (see **3.3.4** above).

Example

Olivia's tax return includes a statement which clearly sets out the facts of a transaction on which Olivia has decided not to pay any tax. Nevertheless, the correct view of the law is unclear and there is sufficient information in that statement to justify an HMRC officer reaching a different view and determining how much additional tax might be payable.

Subject to the comments below, Olivia's statement should preclude an assessment being justified by reference to the test in s. 29(5).

This appears to be borne out by much of the case law, with the single exception of the Court of Appeal's decision in *Sanderson*. Furthermore, if one interprets "discover" as "become aware", this parity of meaning becomes obvious. In addition, it recognises the clear relationship between the under-assessment (the situation in subsection (1)) and the right to make a discovery assessment; it also ensures that there is a fair balance between the rights of HMRC and a taxpayer's entitlement to finality.

The difficulty is that the *Sanderson* decision is binding on the tribunals.

According to *Sanderson*, awareness imports a higher level of knowledge than a mere discovery, amounting to a firmer level of knowledge. What *Sanderson* does not explain is how firm that knowledge must be – given that certainty can rarely be assured.

That said, later cases appear to have adopted a less controversial approach.

Cases: *Sanderson v HMRC* [2016] EWCA Civ 19; *Sheth v HMRC* [2023] UKFTT 368 (TC)

6.7   The case law

6.7.1   Langham v Veltema

Although the case is regularly cited by HMRC, its relevance nowadays is really limited to the single (and now not disputed) question as to what information may be attributed to the hypothetical officer (as discussed at **6.5.2** above).

Furthermore, there are phrases in the lead judgment of Auld LJ which, whilst not inaccurate, are susceptible to misunderstanding, especially if taken out of context.

Case: *Langham (HM Inspector of Taxes) v Veltema* [2004] EWCA Civ 193

6.7.2 Corbally-Stourton

The *Corbally-Stourton* decision now suffers from having been subject to some "polite disapproval" in *Lansdowne Partners*. However, in truth (whilst the author would dispute the overall outcome) the case is a model in explaining the meaning of the various provisions in s. 29 (both those long-standing requirements for a discovery and the new safeguards for the self-assessment era) and their inter-relationship.

In particular, the decision puts beyond doubt the Special Commissioner's view that the level of knowledge relevant for the purposes of s. 29(5) is identical to that needed to justify an assessment generally (a view that is further endorsed in *Lansdowne Partners* – see further below).

Furthermore, the decision gives a clear (and wholly sensible) explanation of the phrase "actual insufficiency" as employed by Auld LJ in *Langham v Veltema* and repeated in a subsequent decision of Henderson J (as he then was) in *Household*:

> "Auld LJ's and Henderson J's judgments use the phrase "actual insufficiency". Only if the inspector is objectively aware at the relevant time of an actual insufficiency is he to be shut out from a discovery assessment. Mr Barnett asks whether this means that, contrary to the view I have expressed at paragraph 46 above, the inspector is only shut out where he is objectively aware that there truly is a certain insufficiency.
>
> I do not understand the judgment in that way. Auld LJ is considering the contrast between an actual insufficiency and a possible insufficiency (an awareness that [the assessment] was questionable): it seems to me that an "actual insufficiency" is used to describe the complement of "an awareness that it was questionable", and accordingly embraces a range of conclusions from absolute certainty to on balance probability, but excludes a conclusion that the insufficiency was merely suspected or "possible" or the sufficiency merely questionable. It does not therefore seem to me that my conclusion at paragraph 46 above is at variance with the views expressed in those judgments."

As noted, the decision was subject to some modest criticism in *Lansdowne Partners*. However, that criticism was limited to one narrow aspect, being the precise formulation of the requisite level of knowledge that would justify an assessment (see **3.3.4** above and **6.7.3** below).

Cases: *HMRC v Household Estate Agents Ltd* [2007] EWHC 1684 (Ch); *Corbally-Stourton v HMRC* (2008) Sp C 692

6.7.3   Lansdowne Partners

At the heart of *Lansdowne Partners* is the application of the s. 29(5) test by reference to ongoing correspondence between HMRC and the taxpayer. However, of particular significance is how the various judges (both at High Court level and in the Court of Appeal) dealt with the level of knowledge (i.e. the practical meaning of "aware") in s. 29(5).

In short, they made it clear that it was to be equated the same level of knowledge that would justify an assessment in the real world. In other words, given a specific set of facts before the hypothetical officer, the s. 29(5) condition is met only if a real-life officer could not have justified on those facts alone a conclusion that there was an under-assessment.

This approach confirms the parity between the two tests as implied by the Special Commissioner in *Corbally-Stourton* and also ensures that the test provides a balance between HMRC and a taxpayer's entitlement to finality.

The relevant passages from the judgments are worthy of note. In the High Court, Lewison J (as he then was) held as follows (with emphasis added):

> "In *Corbally-Stourton* ... the Special Commissioner said that in order to make a discovery the officer need not be certain beyond all doubt that there is an insufficiency: what is required is that he comes to the conclusion on the information available to him and the law as he understands it that it is more likely than not that there is an insufficiency. This approach was adopted by Lord Bannatyne in the Scottish case of *Pattullo*. Mr Coleman [Counsel for HMRC] said that this was the wrong test. HMRC had to know with reasonable certainty of the insufficiency in question otherwise the office could not have been "aware" of it. There is, no doubt, an epistemological debate to be had about whether you can discover or be aware

105

of something that does not in fact exist. In the present case, for example, the [General] Commissioners decided that there was no insufficiency. Had HMRC discovered or been aware of an insufficiency before their decision that there was in fact no insufficiency? Or had they been aware of it, but then ceased to be aware of it? And now that I have disagreed with the Commissioners on one of the points, are HMRC aware of it again? Or have they been aware of it throughout? But I do not consider that I need to enter into this debate. *In the present case the Commissioners asked whether HMRC had sufficient information to make a decision whether to raise an additional assessment. That seems to me to be the right test.*"

The approach seems to have been accepted by the Court of Appeal. For example, the Chancellor of the High Court (Sir Andrew Morritt) held:

"In the end, this part of the appeal boils down to a very short point. The question, to adopt the formulation used by Auld LJ, is whether the hypothetical inspector having before him those three documents and the note of the meeting held on 22nd February 2006 would have been aware of "an actual insufficiency" in the declared profit. I would answer that question in the affirmative. ...

I do not suggest that the hypothetical inspector is required to resolve points of law. Nor need he forecast and discount what the response of the taxpayer may be. It is enough that the information made available to him justifies the amendment to the tax return he then seeks to make. Any disputes of fact or law can then be resolved by the usual processes. For these reasons I would dismiss the appeal of HMRC."

In addition, Moses LJ added the following:

"As the Chancellor points out, awareness of an insufficiency does not require resolution of any potential dispute. After all, once an amendment is made, it may turn out after complex debate in a succession of appeals as to the facts or law, that the profits stated were not insufficient. ...

The statutory context of the condition is the grant of a power to raise an assessment. In that context, the question is whether the taxpayer has provided sufficient information to an officer, with such understanding as he might reasonably be expected to have, to justify the exercise of the power to raise the assessment to make good the insufficiency."

The third judge (Patten LJ) gave the following brief concurring judgment:

"I agree with both judgments."

It is noteworthy that Patten LJ was one of the three judges who later heard *Sanderson* (see **6.7.6** below).

Cases: *HMRC v Lansdowne Partners LP* [2010] EWHC 2582 (Ch); *HMRC v Lansdowne Partners LP* [2011] EWCA Civ 1578

Other aspects of Lansdowne Partners

There are two further aspects of Moses LJ's judgment which should be added for completeness.

First, which simply underlines the point made in the previous paragraph, Moses LJ considered that there might be some circumstances in which even full disclosure of the facts might not give the taxpayer the protection conferred by s. 29(5). As his lordship said:

"I wish to leave open the possibility that, even where the taxpayer has disclosed enough factual information, there may be circumstances in which an officer could not reasonably be expected to be aware of an insufficiency by reason of the complexity of the relevant law."

HMRC have since then regularly seized upon these words and argued in subsequent cases that the facts of those subsequent cases were complex and therefore did not confer any protection on the taxpayer. It should be noted, however, that the words of Moses LJ were simply to keep open the possibility in some future exceptional case that even full disclosure would not keep a case outside s. 29(5). Indeed, as subsequently noted by the Upper Tribunal in *Charlton*:

"That is not to say that there might not be cases where the complexity of the relevant law would lead to a conclusion that, even where the taxpayer has disclosed enough factual information, such a hypothetical officer could not reasonably be expected to be aware of an insufficiency. That was the view expressed by Moses LJ in *Lansdowne*. In that case the court found that the legal points were not complex or difficult. But we find support for our view that complexity or difficulty should not routinely present an obstacle (as they would if all specialist knowledge had to be assumed away) from the fact that Moses LJ considered this only to be a mere possibility, and thus at most an exception and not the rule."

The second further aspect arising from the judgment is the judge's polite disapproval of the wording adopted by the Special Commissioner in *Corbally-Stourton*. The Special Commissioner had described the level of knowledge necessary to justify an assessment as an officer believing that it was more likely than not that there was an under-assessment. Moses LJ responded as follows:

"I think there is a danger in substituting wording appropriate to standards of proof for the statutory condition. The statutory condition turns on the situation of which the officer could reasonably have been expected to be aware. Awareness is a matter of perception and of understanding, not of conclusion. I wish, therefore, to express doubt as to the approach of the Special Commissioner in *Corbally-Stourton* and of the Outer House in *Pattullo*, namely, that to be aware of a situation is the same as concluding that it is more probable than not. The statutory context of the condition is the grant of a power to raise an assessment."

That final sentence further emphasises the key point being that the s. 29(5) threshold should be the same as that which applies for s. 29(1).

See also **3.3.4** above.

Cases: *HMRC v Lansdowne Partners LP* [2011] EWCA Civ 1578; *HMRC v Charlton (and others)* [2012] UKUT 770 (TCC)

6.7.4   *Charlton*

The *Charlton* case effectively built on the *Lansdowne* decision in the slightly less attractive context of an avoidance scheme. It will be remembered, of course, that the statute does not distinguish between different kinds of situation and, therefore, there is no reason why tax avoidance cases ought to be considered any differently. This indeed seems to be borne out by the *Charlton* case.

The most significant aspect of the decision (in the context of s. 29(5)) is that it provides clear authority for the proposition that the skills and knowledge of the hypothetical officer are dependent on the information deemed to be before him or her (see the discussion at **6.3** above). The case also provides authority on the interpretation of the reasonable inference test in s. 29(6)(d) (see **6.5.3** above). Furthermore, the case is a good modern authority on the meaning of discovery (see **3.3** and **3.9** above).

The practical upshot of the case was that a line-by-line explanation of the transactions in the white space of the taxpayers' returns was considered to be sufficient to have made the hypothetical officer aware that the taxpayer's treatment was different from how HMRC would have treated those transactions. (Although the officer was also deemed to have the DOTAS disclosure, the Upper Tribunal made it clear that it would have reached the same conclusion even if the DOTAS material had been excluded.)

In particular, the Upper Tribunal considered that (contrary to HMRC's guidance), it was not necessary for a taxpayer to include an express statement to the effect that a different stance had been taken:

> "We do not accept that there is any overriding requirement that the information has to explain how the scheme works (although in this case we consider that would in any event be met by the availability of the form AAG1), nor that the information must specify, if it be the case, that the view adopted by the taxpayer is different from that taken by HMRC."

Case: *HMRC v Charlton (and others)* [2012] UKUT 770 (TCC)

6.7.5   Pattullo

The *Pattullo* case, however, came to a different outcome from that in *Charlton*, despite a similar level of disclosure. The only practical difference between the two cases is that the events in *Pattullo* actually predated those in *Charlton* and that at the relevant date (i.e. the last date on which an enquiry could have been opened into the relevant returns):

- in *Pattullo*, there was no court or tribunal decision to highlight the fact that the underlying scheme might not work; whereas

- in *Charlton*, the hypothetical officer would have had the benefit of a decision of the Special Commissioners and the High Court.

In the author's view, that difference (which might be sufficient in some cases) was not sufficient to justify two different outcomes. Furthermore, the *Charlton* decision should be favoured because there will be plenty of cases when an officer has to form a decision to make an assessment without there being a specific precedent on which to base his decision.

Another difficulty that the author has with the *Pattullo* decision is the fact that the judge appears to have concluded that the hypothetical officer could not have been expected to have read HMRC's own guidance manuals. The taxpayer had claimed a capital loss on a capital redemption policy, contrary to HMRC's own published (albeit incorrect) views that such policies are outside the scope of CGT (and therefore no allowable losses could arise).

Cases: *HMRC v Charlton (and others)* [2012] UKUT 770 (TCC); *Pattullo v HMRC* [2016] UKUT 270 (TCC)

6.7.6   Sanderson

The greatest threat to the meaningfulness of s. 29(5) as a protection for a taxpayer, however, was the Court of Appeal's decision in *Sanderson*.

In many ways, the case is similar to *Charlton* in which a white-space disclosure set out the transactions that formed part of a tax avoidance scheme. One distinction is that (unbeknown to the taxpayer) the transactions had not been properly implemented, and so what the taxpayer thought had happened did not. The scheme therefore failed due to implementation errors rather than on technical grounds.

Leaving aside the fact that the taxpayer advanced arguments to the effect that (in the unusual circumstances of the case) the hypothetical officer ought to have known about the implementation failings, a taxpayer cannot usually rely on a disclosed set of facts that did not in the end take place. This is because the hypothetical officer's knowledge is generally limited to what is disclosed. However, the taxpayer argued that there was sufficient information in the disclosure that would have justified an assessment (on the basis that HMRC could have put forward the argument that the scheme – had it been properly implemented – fell down on technical grounds as well). The Court of Appeal, although it is not expressly stated, implied that it agreed with this analysis. The case, however, focused on the level of knowledge that applies for the purposes of the s. 29(5) test:

> "Mr Sanderson's case is that the Upper Tribunal over-stated the level of knowledge which needs to be imputed to the officer under s.29(5) in order to justify the making of a discovery assessment. The threshold is said to be a relatively low one and merely requires the officer to be able to justify his belief that further tax is due. Part of [Counsel's] argument rests on eliding the requirement in s.29(1) for an officer to "discover" that there is an insufficiency in the return with the condition in s.29(5) that the notional officer could not have been reasonably expected, on the information available, to be "aware" of that insufficiency. Unless, it is said, the threshold of knowledge is set relatively low it would be difficult, if not impossible, in most cases for the Revenue to be able to raise an assessment under s.29(1).
>
> I do not accept that ss.29(1) and (5) import the same test and that the Revenue's power to raise an assessment is therefore directly dependent on the level of awareness which the notional officer would have based on the s.29(6) information. The exercise of the s.29(1) power is made by a real officer who is required to come to a conclusion about a possible insufficiency based on all the available information at the time when the discovery assessment is made. Section 29(5) operates to place a restriction on the exercise of that power by reference to a hypothetical officer who is required to carry out an evaluation of the adequacy of the return at a fixed and different point in time on the basis of a fixed and limited class of information. The purpose of the condition is to test the adequacy of the taxpayer's disclosure, not to prescribe the circumstances which would justify the real officer in exercising the s.29(1) power. Although there will inevitably be points of

contact between the real and the hypothetical exercises which ss.29(1) and (5) involve, the tests are not the same."

Although the judge made reference to the earlier decision in *Lansdowne Partners*, the author, with respect, cannot see how the two judgments can be reconciled. Nevertheless, permission to appeal was refused by the Supreme Court and therefore the decision must be considered to be final.

It should be noted that the cross-over of commentary on s. 29(1) and (5) was nevertheless recognised by the FTT in *Clark*.

Cases: *Sanderson v HMRC* [2016] EWCA Civ 19; *Clark v HMRC* [2017] UKFTT 392 (TC)

6.7.7 *Cooke*

The conflicting case law was considered in *Cooke*. Ultimately, though, the tribunal felt that a decision could be reached on the facts without determining the precise legal test. This was because the fact of the excessive foreign tax credits claimed was obvious from the tax returns themselves.

Case: *Cooke v HMRC* [2017] UKFTT 844 (TC)

6.7.8 *Hicks*

In *Hicks*, the FTT also expressly acknowledged the difficulties in understanding or applying the *Sanderson* analysis, saying that it left the key issue "opaque". Similarly, the wording "actual insufficiency" from *Langham v Veltema* which was endorsed in *Sanderson* was not considered to be "helpful". Given the apparent departure from the approach set out in *Lansdowne*, the tribunal felt that the result of the *Sanderson* judgment was to make it clear what the test was not, and not what the test is.

Following HMRC's appeal, the Upper Tribunal then had an opportunity to set out its own understanding of the approach required for the purposes of s. 29(5), as follows:

> "193. The FTT ... emphasised the importance in the application of section 29(5) of the quality of the taxpayer's disclosure. As the FTT said: "Subsection (5) is all about disclosure by the taxpayer (as defined by section 29(6))." We consider this to be a correct statement and it discloses no error

of law. If we may respectfully make a criticism of some of the earlier case-law it is that there has been an undue focus on the expertise, the technical knowledge of, the availability of HMRC Manuals to and the availability of specialist advice to the hypothetical inspector. That represents a misunderstanding of the purpose of section 29(5).

194.   In our judgment, section 29(5) requires that a taxpayer should make sufficient disclosure in order to enable an officer to make an informed decision whether an insufficiency existed sufficient to justify, in the words of Moses LJ [in *Lansdowne* at [69]], the exercise of the power to make an amendment to the return. We respectfully agree with Moses LJ that the possibility should remain open that mere factual disclosure may not, in some cases involving complex issues of law, be sufficient.

195.   The purpose of section 29(5) is to strike a balance between the protection of the revenue, on the one hand, and the taxpayer on the other. The taxpayer is protected against a discovery assessment provided adequate disclosure has been made. The disclosure must be from the sources referred to in section 29(6) (as amplified by section 29(7)). HMRC are protected because they can raise a discovery assessment if adequate disclosure has not been made.

196.   It seems to us that section 29(5) focuses primarily on the adequacy of the disclosure by the taxpayer. What constitutes adequate disclosure for the purposes of section 29(5) will vary from case to case. It depends on the nature and tax implications of the arrangements concerned and not on the assumed knowledge (or lack of knowledge) of the hypothetical officer. The obligation is on the taxpayer to make the appropriate level of disclosure as befits a self-assessment system.

197.   In a relatively simple case, where the legal principles are clear, it would be sufficient for a taxpayer simply to give a full disclosure of the factual position. The return must also make clear what position the taxpayer is adopting in relation to the factual position (e.g. whether a receipt was not taxable or whether a claim for relief was being made).

198.   But there may be other cases where the law and the facts (and/or the relationship between the law and the facts) are so complex that adequate disclosure may require more than pure factual disclosure: namely some adequate explanation of the main tax law issues raised by the facts and the position taken in respect of those issues.

199.   Plainly, the greater the level of disclosure, the greater the officer's awareness can reasonably be expected to be. If a disclosure on a tax return includes all material facts and, in complex cases, an adequate explanation of the technical issues raised by those facts and the position taken in relation to those issues, it would be reasonable to expect an officer to be aware of an insufficiency. What constitutes reasonable awareness is linked to the fullness and adequacy of the disclosure – the expertise of the hypothetical officer remains that of general competence, knowledge or skill which includes a reasonable knowledge and understanding of the law.

200.   In argument before us [Counsel for HMRC] came close to suggesting, as we understood it, that a hypothetical officer could not be expected to understand complex or specialist areas of tax law. We disagree. If the disclosure (factual and technical) is adequate in the circumstances of the case, a hypothetical officer can reasonably be expected to be aware of an insufficiency even in a complex case or one involving specialist technical knowledge. If the disclosure is inadequate then it is fair that a hypothetical officer could not reasonably be expected to be aware of an insufficiency in such a case. That is the balance that section 29(5) strikes."

Cases: *Hicks v HMRC* [2018] UKFTT 22 (TC); *HMRC v Hicks* [2020] UKUT 12 (TCC)

6.7.9   *Beagles*

In the meantime, the Upper Tribunal in *Beagles* set out its own summary, based on what had been said in *Sanderson*:

"(1)   The test in s29(5) is applied by reference to a hypothetical HMRC officer not the actual officer in the case. The officer has the characteristics of an officer of general competence, knowledge or skill which include a reasonable knowledge and understanding of the law.

(2)   The test requires the court or tribunal to identify the information that is treated by s29(6) as available to the hypothetical officer at the relevant time and determine whether on the basis of that information the hypothetical officer applying that level of knowledge and skill could not have been reasonably expected to be aware of the insufficiency.

(3)   The hypothetical officer is expected to apply his knowledge of the law to the facts disclosed to form a view as to whether or not an insufficiency exists (Moses LJ, *Lansdowne* [69]; Patten LJ, *Sanderson* [23]). We agree therefore with Mr Firth that the test does assume that the hypothetical officer will apply the appropriate level of knowledge and skill to the information that is treated as being available before the level of awareness is tested. The test does not require that the actual insufficiency is identified on the face of the return.

(4)   But the question of the knowledge of the hypothetical officer cuts both ways. He or she is not expected to resolve every question of law particularly in complex cases (Patten LJ, *Sanderson* [23], *Lansdowne* [69]). In some cases, it may be that the law is so complex that the inspector could not reasonably have been expected to be aware of the insufficiency (Moses LJ, *Lansdowne* [69]; Patten LJ, *Sanderson* [17(3)]).

(5)   The hypothetical officer must be aware of the actual insufficiency from the information that is treated as available by s29(6) (Auld LJ, *Langham v Veltema* [33] [34]; Patten LJ, *Sanderson* [22]). The information need not be sufficient to enable HMRC to prove its case (Moses LJ, *Lansdowne* [69]) but it must be more than would prompt the hypothetical officer to raise an enquiry (Auld LJ, *Langham v Veltema* [33]; Patten LJ, *Sanderson* [35]).

(6)   As can be seen from the discussion in *Sanderson* (see [23]), the level of awareness is a question of judgment not a particular standard of proof (see also Moses LJ in *Lansdowne* [70]). The information made available must "justify" raising the additional assessment (Moses LJ, *Lansdowne* [69]) or be sufficient to enable HMRC to make a decision whether to raise

115

an additional assessment (Lewison J in the High Court in *Lansdowne* [2011] BTC 224 at [48])."

Case: *Beagles v HMRC* [2018] UKUT 380 (TCC)

6.7.10   Ball Europe Ltd

Ball Europe Ltd concerned a gain disclosed in a company's statement of recognised gains and losses, and associated notes, but which did not form a part of the company's profit as calculated in the profit and loss account.

Applying the guidance given in *Beagles* (see **6.7.9**), the tribunal made the following observations:

- the hypothetical officer is imputed with knowledge other than tax law;
- moreover, the hypothetical officer is imputed with sufficient knowledge to understand and interpret disclosures made in a company's accounts which accompany a tax return, all the more so given the long-established alignment of accounting and tax law; and
- such knowledge was distinguished from the non-core property valuation expertise that was the issue in *Langham v Veltema*.

Applying those principles to the facts of the case, the tribunal considered that the hypothetical officer would have appreciated that:

- not all of a company's taxable income is reflected in the profit and loss account;
- something found in the capital or reserves section of a company's accounts might still be taxable;
- if something is not income, but is a gain, it is likely to be taxed as "derived from an asset" under TCGA 1992 rules in the UK, which have a wide scope – this was described as "basic tax law"; and
- there is (formerly known as Schedule D, Case VI) a "catch-all" tax charge for matters not otherwise subject to tax.

At that stage, the tribunal found that there was sufficient information at least to make the hypothetical officer carry out a more detailed investigation. That on its own would not be enough to invalidate the discovery assessment. Accordingly, the tribunal proceeded to consider whether the hypothetical officer should reasonably have been expected to be aware of the under-assessment. In its further analysis, the tribunal noted:

- this was not a complex case as alluded to in *Lansdowne* and *Sanderson*; but instead
- "it is much more straightforward to identify a sum stated in the accounts and decide whether it is taxable or not".

The tribunal concluded as follows:

"it must have been clear that the £10,812,449 ought to be chargeable under at least one of the potential heads of charge identified. This would be enough information to enable our hypothetical officer to have decided to raise an assessment either under one of cases [III or VI of Schedule D] or as a capital gain, even if at this stage he or she could not identify which of those was the more technically correct basis for a tax charge."

Accordingly, the appeal was allowed.

Case: *Ball Europe Ltd v HMRC* [2021] UKFTT 23 (TC)

6.7.11   Carter & Kennedy

Carter & Kennedy involved an SDLT scheme in relation to a couple's purchase of a residential property. The scheme involved taking advantage of the sub-sale rules but, given latter case law developments, would probably have fallen foul of a widely drafted anti-avoidance provision.

A disclosure note sent to HMRC at the same time as the land tax return identified the sub-sale and also raised, but then dismissed, the possible relevance of the anti-avoidance provision.

The FTT set out its own formulation of the principles as follows:

"(1)   The objective awareness test relates to the adequacy of the disclosure that has been made by the taxpayer. The test requires the court or tribunal to identify the information that is treated as available at the relevant time and determine, whether, on the basis of that information, a hypothetical officer could not have been reasonably expected to be aware of the insufficiency.

(2)   It is necessary to bear in mind the general principle that HMRC is only to be prevented from making a discovery assessment where the taxpayer "in making an honest and accurate return … [has] clearly alerted [HMRC] to the insufficiency of the assessment".

(3)   If the level of disclosure is to prevent the issue of an assessment by HMRC, the information that is treated as available at the relevant time must be sufficient as to make the hypothetical officer aware of the actual insufficiency to a level that would justify the making of an assessment. The information need not be sufficient to enable HMRC to prove its case, but it is not enough that the information might prompt the hypothetical officer to raise an enquiry.

(4)   The hypothetical officer should be treated as being of general competence, knowledge or skill, which includes a reasonable knowledge and understanding of the law. In determining the adequacy of the disclosure, it can be assumed that the hypothetical officer will apply his or her knowledge of the law to the facts disclosed and to form a view as to whether or not an insufficiency exists."

It added by noting that the knowledge of the hypothetical officer was not fixed. Instead:

"the level of awareness and knowledge that [the] inspector is expected to apply to the information … may well change over time".

As to the relationship of the knowledge of the actual enquiring officer and the hypothetical officer, the FTT noted:

"The test is performed by reference to a hypothetical officer not an actual HMRC officer such as Mr Kane. That having been said, I do take into account his evidence in considering the general level of awareness that it is reasonable to ascribe to the hypothetical officer when reviewing the information that is treated as available to the officer by paragraph 30(4). In doing so, I take into account that Mr Kane is a specialist and was at the forefront of HMRC's efforts to counteract these schemes and so his technical knowledge was likely to be more advanced than might reasonably be expected of officers within HMRC in general. But I also take into account that, as I have mentioned above, the hypothetical officer is not required to resolve all issues or ... every question of law. The test is simply whether the information available would justify the HMRC officer in raising an assessment. ...

I would expect a hypothetical officer of general competence, knowledge or skill at the time who was reviewing the SD[L]T1 return and the disclosure note to be aware of s75A FA 2003 and of its potential application to counteract tax avoidance schemes. However, at the time, the inspector would be in some doubt about the scope of s75A FA 2003. It was not until some time later (in 2013) that this tribunal first heard the appeal in the case, which led to the Supreme Court decision in *Project Blue Limited v Revenue and Customs Commissioners* [2018] UKSC 30. The reference in the disclosure note to s75A, it seems to me, would have prompted further investigation, but without further explanation would not have led the inspector to an awareness of a loss of tax."

Applying those principles, the FTT took the view that the level of disclosure was not sufficient to make a hypothetical officer aware of the potential under-assessment, asserting that the case was "relatively complex". Accordingly, the tribunal dismissed the appeal.

The Upper Tribunal, on the taxpayers' appeal, noted that neither party sought to disagree with the principles as set out by the FTT. The Upper Tribunal emphasised that it was not in a position to remake the decision, simply because it might have interpreted the facts differently. The test on the adequacy of a disclosure is for the FTT to make and the Upper Tribunal can intervene only if an error of approach has been made (or the FTT's finding is one that no reasonable FTT could have made). The taxpayers' appeal was therefore dismissed.

Cases: *Carter & Kennedy v HMRC* [2020] UKFTT 179 (TC); *Carter & Kennedy v HMRC* [2021] UKUT 300 (TCC)

6.8 Other taxes

6.8.1 Corporation tax

The equivalent provisions are found in FA 1998, Sch. 18, para. 44. The only difference is that the corporation tax rules make no reference to non-resident CGT tax returns.

Law: FA 1998, Sch. 18, para. 44

6.8.2 SDLT

The equivalent provisions are found in FA 2003, Sch. 10, para. 30(3), (4).

The SDLT rules similarly make no reference to non-resident CGT returns. In fact, the only tax return that is deemed to be before the hypothetical officer is the SDLT return itself. Similarly, the hypothetical officer is not deemed to have any information concerning any claim made by the taxpayer (other than what is on the SDLT return itself).

Law: FA 2003, Sch. 10, para. 30(3), (4)

6.8.3 ATED

The equivalent provisions are found in FA 2013, Sch. 33, para. 24(3)-(5).

The ATED rules similarly make no reference to non-resident CGT returns. Also, as with SDLT, the only tax return that is deemed to be before the hypothetical officer is the ATED return itself. Similarly, the hypothetical officer is not deemed to have any information concerning any claim made by the taxpayer (other than what is on the ATED return itself).

Law: FA 2013, Sch. 33, para. 24(3)-(5)

6.9   Other discovery provisions

6.9.1   Non-resident capital gains tax

The equivalent provisions

Although the provisions do not apply to tax years after 2018-19, the potential for a discovery assessment in respect of an earlier period remains.

The equivalent provisions are found in TMA 1970, s. 29A(5)-(7).

In non-resident CGT cases, the hypothetical officer is deemed to be in possession of material relating to both self-assessment tax returns and non-resident CGT returns for the tax year in question as well as in relation to the two previous tax years.

Law: TMA 1970, s. 29A(5)-(7)

6.9.2   Partnership returns

The equivalent provisions

The equivalent provisions are found in TMA 1970, s. 30B(6). Section 30B(7) expressly applies the rules otherwise applying for income tax and CGT to partnership cases.

Law: TMA 1970, s. 30B(6), (7)

7.   Defences against a discovery assessment

7.1   Introduction

In practice, the arguments about whether or not a discovery has been made and those concerning careless or deliberate conduct and the quality of the disclosure (see **Chapters 3, 5** and **6** above) are used by taxpayers as a defence against a discovery assessment. The same is the case when it comes to time limits (see **Chapter 8** below). Strictly speaking, however, they are all conditions that HMRC need to satisfy in order for a discovery assessment to be valid.

This point is further emphasised by the Upper Tribunal's decision in *Burgess/Brimheath*, which made clear that HMRC are obliged to demonstrate the validity of the assessment, showing that each statutory condition is met.

Nevertheless, the statute does contain an express further defence which can be deployed by taxpayers in order to defeat an otherwise competent discovery assessment. This is the prevailing practice defence discussed below.

Of course, the taxpayer can also challenge the amount or even the fact of assessment by arguing that the officer's conclusion that there is an under-assessment is simply wrong (or that the amount assessed is wrong).

In *Ashraf*, the tribunal allowed an appeal against a discovery assessment on the basis that it wrongly described the under-assessed amount as "miscellaneous income".

Cases: *Burgess v HMRC, Brimheath Developments Ltd v HMRC* [2015] UKUT 578 (TCC); *Ashraf v HMRC* [2018] UKFTT 97 (TC)

7.2   Prevailing practice defence

7.2.1   Overview

The prevailing practice defence is to ensure that a discovery assessment may not be made simply as a result of a development in the law which either makes an earlier assessment deficient or highlights a deficiency in an earlier assessment which was not otherwise appreciated. Similarly, it ensures that a change of HMRC practice (even if justified) cannot be retrospectively applied via a discovery assessment.

This is a further example of where discovery assessments are more onerous than enquiries for HMRC. When issuing a closure notice at the end of an enquiry, HMRC may apply any new case law or practice, even if the tax return (when originally submitted) fully complied with the prevailing practice at the time. However, once the enquiry window is closed, the taxpayer should be protected from any change of approach by HMRC.

There are three conditions which need to be satisfied if a taxpayer is to rely on this defence:

- the taxpayer must have made and delivered a tax return for the relevant tax year;
- the under-assessment must be attributable to an error or mistake in the return as to the basis on which the taxpayer's liability ought to have been computed; and
- the return was made on the basis or in accordance with the practice generally prevailing at the time when the return was made.

The defence is to be extended to cover returns under Making Tax Digital (currently with effect from 6 April 2024).

Law: TMA 1970, s. 29(2); SI 2021/1079, reg. 2

7.2.2   Tax return made and delivered

This first condition is straightforward. Furthermore, it is an obvious condition given that the third condition also depends on the return having been made. Even questions about the validity of the return are now academic following the enactment of TMA 1970, s. 12D (see **5.2.2**).

Law: TMA 1970, s. 12D

7.2.3   Types of error

The second condition appears to ensure that the error in the return has to have reflected a misunderstanding as to how the taxpayer's liability ought to have been computed. For example, a simple arithmetical error would seem to be excluded from this defence.

If this is the case, then it seems that the second condition adds very little to the test given the stringent terms laid down by the third condition discussed below.

7.2.4   *Prevailing practice*

The third condition compares the methodology behind the tax return with "the practice generally prevailing" when the return was made.

In *Hargreaves*, the taxpayer pointed out that the return has to have been made "on the basis or in accordance with the practice generally prevailing". He argued that the word "or" meant that a taxpayer had two separate routes to come within the terms of this third condition. However, the Upper Tribunal considered that the word "or" was to address two mutually exclusive situations:

- those where a tax return is prepared with a particular practice in mind ("on the basis ..."); and
- those where a tax return is prepared without knowledge of any particular practice but nevertheless in accordance with the practice generally prevailing ("in accordance with ...").

In *Jacobs*, the tribunal concluded that it was not necessary to focus on the precise methodology for preparing tax returns: instead it was the underlying principles that were important. As the tribunal ruled:

> "HMRC formulated this as 'it was not current practice not to account for associated companies in tax returns'. Our view is that the current prevailing practice referred to is less the way in which a return was filled in, than the then current understanding of the law on which that return was based ..."

Cases: *Jacobs Construction (Holdings) Ltd v HMRC* [2016] UKFTT 555 (TC); *HMRC v Hargreaves* [2022] UKUT 34 (TCC)

Whose practice?

It is clear that there must be at least a broad body of support for a practice to be generally prevailing. As the Upper Tribunal held in *Moore*:

> "However, Mr Moore's supplementary argument that what he did – which had been his habit over several years – was a "generally prevailing" practice which brought him within the protection of s 29(2), does not have the same merit and I

> should perhaps deal with it immediately. The "generally prevailing" practice at which sub-s (2) is aimed is quite obviously one commonly adopted by taxpayers in general at any given time, and not an idiosyncratic practice adopted by a single taxpayer, however frequently he may have done so."

The combination of words "generally" and "prevailing" are, however, susceptible to different interpretations. The author considers that it requires the practice to be firmly established but does not require a universally accepted practice. The words would suggest a threshold higher than 50%. However, this would be nigh on impossible to prove (and/or for the tribunal to verify) and so it is unlikely to have been intended by Parliament.

However, in *Household*, it was held that a practice had to be:

> "relatively   long-established,   readily   ascertainable   by interested parties, and accepted by HMRC and taxpayers' advisers alike".

This was subsequently endorsed in *Moore*.

The question that arises, therefore, is the extent to which HMRC's "views" can amount or contribute to the prevailing practice. Of course, HMRC can shape the practice. But what impact do they have on the question as to whether a practice is "generally prevailing"? After all, they do not have a "practice" as required by the statutory test.

Part of the difficulty arises from the fact that *Household* relied upon a decision of the Special Commissioners which concerned a slightly different test and in a wholly different context.

On balance, the author considers that (if available) HMRC's view of the law is a relevant factor, but (contrary to the view expressed in *Household*) is not a critical component of showing what amounts to the practice generally prevailing: it is what taxpayers (and their advisers) generally believed the law to be which is the true test.

Cases: *HMRC v Household Estate Agents Ltd* [2007] EWHC 1684 (Ch); *Moore v HMRC* [2011] UKUT 239 (TCC)

Interaction with other conditions for a discovery assessment

On a straightforward reading of the statute, the prevailing practice defence is equally applicable irrespective of whether HMRC are relying on careless/deliberate conduct or on an insufficient disclosure. However, as noted in *Daniel*, the relevance of the prevailing practice defence is likely to be more limited in the former scenario.

In particular, demonstrating a widespread practice (even if not the practice generally prevailing) is likely to counter any suggestion by HMRC that the taxpayer had been careless. Furthermore, the conditions for the defence are almost certainly inapplicable in any case of deliberate conduct. As a result, the practical application of the defence is most likely limited to those cases where HMRC are relying on insufficiency of disclosure.

Case: *Daniel v HMRC* [2014] UKFTT 173 (TC)

7.3   Other taxes

7.3.1   Corporation tax

The equivalent provisions are found in FA 1998, Sch. 18, para. 45.

7.3.2   SDLT

The equivalent provisions are found in FA 2003, Sch. 10, para. 30(5).

7.3.3   ATED

The equivalent provisions are found in FA 2013, Sch. 33, para. 24(7).

7.3.4   Digital services tax

The equivalent provision in relation to the public interest business protection tax is found in FA 2020, Sch. 8, para. 20(5).

7.3.5   Public interest business protection tax

There is no equivalent provision in relation to the public interest business protection tax.

7.3.6   Multinational top-up tax

The equivalent provision in relation to the multinational top-up tax is found in F(No. 2)A 2023, Sch. 14, para. 28(6).

7.4   Other discovery provisions

7.4.1   Non-resident capital gains tax

There was no prevailing practice defence available in the case of discovery determinations made for non-resident CGT.

7.4.2   Partnership returns

The equivalent provisions

The equivalent provision is found in TMA 1970, s. 30B(3). There is no practical difference between the rules for partnerships and those otherwise applying for income tax and CGT.

Law: TMA 1970, s. 30B(3)

8. Time limits for discovery assessments

8.1 Introduction

8.1.1 *Overview*

Even if public law obligations on HMRC (or, previously, the issue of staleness) mean that an assessment should not be made unreasonably long after the discovery (see **3.9.6** above), statute provides absolute time limits for any assessment. If the assessment is made too late, it is invalid.

Under the "requirement to correct" legislation, time limits falling after 5 April 2017 were suspended until 5 April 2021 in respect of offshore matters. However, further extensions were enacted in FA 2019, again in relation to offshore matters (see **8.4**).

8.1.2 *When is an assessment made?*

It should be noted that the critical date is not the date on which the notice of assessment is received by the taxpayer, but the date on which the administrative processes are completed inside HMRC.

Historically, this was the time when the assessment book was completed (*Honig*). For the modern equivalent, the Special Commissioner in *Corbally-Stourton* held that an officer made the assessment:

> "when, having decided to make it, he authorised the entry of its amount into the computer".

A subtly different approach was taken in *Tutty*:

> "The assessment was made, in the modern way, *by entering the details* in the HMRC computer." (emphasis added)

In the VAT case of *Aria*, the Court of Appeal made four observations which are likely to be equally applicable to discovery assessments:

- There is no statutory definition of "assessment". It is in general a legal act on the part of HMRC constituting their determination of the amount of tax due.

- There is no particular formality required by either statute or regulations.

- There is no magic in the use of any particular form, for example one headed "Notice of Assessment". A notification of an assessment can be contained simply in a letter. It can also be contained in more than one document.

- The question whether an assessment has been made or not is to be determined on an objective analysis. The decision-maker's subjective state of mind cannot alter that objective fact.

Although the court emphasised the conceptual distinction between an assessment and a notice of assessment, in many cases there might not be any meaningful distinction between the first three of these principles. The court continued by noting that:

> "It is essential to the fair administration of the tax system that a taxpayer should be able to know with certainty whether or not an assessment has been made of an amount ... due from him. There would be very considerable uncertainty if the question whether an assessment has been made were to depend on the subjective intentions and beliefs of individual officers of HMRC."

Cases: *Honig v Sarsfield (HM Inspector of Taxes)* [1986] STC 246, [1986] BTC 205; *Corbally-Stourton v HMRC* (2008) Sp C 692; *Tutty v HMRC* [2019] UKFTT 3 (TC); *Aria Technology Ltd v HMRC* [2020] EWCA Civ 182

8.2   The time limits

The time limits below operate by reference to the date of the assessment and the tax year to which the assessment relates ("the relevant tax year").

8.2.1   The basic four-year time limit

Since 1 April 2010, there has been a basic time limit of four years from the end of the relevant tax year. Therefore, an assessment for the 2019-20 tax year cannot be out of time if it is made on or before 5 April 2024.

Law: TMA 1970, s. 34(1)

8.2.2   The extended four-year time limit

On certain occasions, income assessable under ITEPA 2003 (employment income, pension income and social security income) may be assessable in a tax year earlier than that in which the income was actually received. In those circumstances, the four-year time limit runs from the end of the tax year in which the income was received.

If the taxpayer has died, there is an overriding time limit of four years from the end of the year of assessment in which the taxpayer died. However, an alternative time limit can also apply in cases of deceased taxpayers (see **8.2.5**).

Law: TMA 1970, s. 35, 40(1)

8.2.3   The six-year time limit in careless conduct cases

HMRC have an additional two years (i.e. until the end of six years after the relevant tax year) if there is a loss of tax brought about carelessly by the taxpayer or a person acting on the taxpayer's behalf.

This is identical to the test in s. 29(4) (see **5.4** above). Consequently, in those cases where the assessment is made more than four years after the end of the relevant tax year, there would be no point in HMRC seeking to justify the assessment under s. 29(5) (and HMRC, sensibly, do not generally bother to try to do so). In *Mullens*, the Upper Tribunal confirmed that no additional burden lay on HMRC to prove, over and above the careless conduct, that there was an *actual* loss of tax. The only additional fact that HMRC would need to prove (if the condition in s. 29(4) has been established) is that the assessment was made within the four-year time limit.

If the taxpayer has died, there is an overriding time limit of four years from the end of the year of assessment in which the taxpayer died. However, an alternative time limit can also apply in cases of deceased taxpayers (see **8.2.5**).

Law: TMA 1970, s. 36(1), (1B), 40(1)
Case: *Mullens v HMRC* [2023] UKUT 244 (TCC)

8.2.4   The 20-year time limit in certain cases

In certain cases, HMRC may make a discovery assessment up to 20 years after the end of the relevant tax year. For this extended time limit to apply, HMRC must show that the loss of income tax or CGT is either:

- brought about deliberately by the taxpayer or a person acting on the taxpayer's behalf;
- attributable to the taxpayer's failure to comply with an obligation to notify HMRC of chargeable income (under TMA 1970, s. 7);
- attributable to arrangements in which the taxpayer has failed to comply with DOTAS notification obligations under FA 2004, s. 309, 310 or 313; or
- attributable to arrangements in which the taxpayer has failed to comply with a POTAS notification obligation under FA 2014, s. 253.

These are discussed further below.

It will be noted that the latter three conditions do not turn on any failures by third parties – only failures by the taxpayer him or herself. Furthermore, statute provides that any reasonable excuse deems the failure not to have occurred. If the reasonable excuse has come to an end, then the previous failure must be remedied without unreasonable delay.

If the taxpayer has died, there is an overriding time limit of four years from the end of the year of assessment in which the taxpayer died. However, an alternative time limit can also apply in cases of deceased taxpayers (see **8.2.5**).

Law: TMA 1970, s. 36(1A), (1B), 40(1), 118(2)

Loss of tax brought about deliberately

This is practically the same test as applies for the purposes of s. 29(4) discussed at **5.6** above.

Given the fact that s. 29(4) turns on "careless *or* deliberate" conduct (and because carelessness is generally easier for HMRC to prove), it is more common for allegations of deliberate conduct to be made only in cases where HMRC are assessing more than six years after the end of the relevant tax year.

Nevertheless, in a case of a clear suppression of income, for example, HMRC would be wise to assert deliberate conduct rather than mere carelessness. This is because taking care to underpay one's tax falls outside the meaning of "failing to take reasonable care". This distinction was implicitly recognised by the tribunal in *Chadburn*.

In *Mullens*, the Upper Tribunal confirmed that no additional burden lay on HMRC to prove, over and above any deliberate conduct, that there was an *actual* loss of tax. The only additional fact that HMRC would need to prove (if the deliberate condition in s. 29(4) has been established) is that the assessment was made within the 20-year time limit. In any case, however, where s. 29(4) does not need to be established (i.e. because no return had been submitted – see **Chapter 4**) then HMRC would be required to prove that there had been deliberate conduct that has caused *a* loss of tax. Again, it is not necessary for HMRC to prove the accuracy of the amount they have assessed, and certainly not that that was the amount of tax lost as a result of the deliberate conduct.

Law: TMA 1970, s. 36(1A)(a)

Cases: *Chadburn v HMRC* [2016] UKFTT 755 (TC); *Mullens v HMRC* [2023] UKUT 244 (TCC)

Failure to notify chargeability

Unless an individual has already been served with a notice to file a tax return under TMA 1970, s. 8, there is a general obligation on individuals to notify HMRC of the fact that taxable income has been received, so that a notice to submit a tax return can be issued. This obligation is found in TMA 1970, s. 7 and requires HMRC to be notified within six months of the end of the relevant tax year (i.e. by the following 5 October).

It should be remembered, however, that s. 7 contains a number of exceptions, principally to excuse individuals from any such notification in cases where their tax affairs can be fully catered for through PAYE. The full workings of the ever-increasingly complex provisions in s. 7 are beyond the scope of this book.

However, the provision in s. 7(3) should not be overlooked. This ensures that any individual subject to any of the freestanding charges to tax listed in ITA 2007, s. 30 (including most notably the high income child benefit charge) is required to notify chargeability and, otherwise, will face a 20-year assessment time limit. (There is currently a debate as to whether the various charges under the pension rules, despite being included within s. 30, are actually subject to this obligation. This is a live matter being considered by the tribunals.)

On the other hand, simply failing to comply with the provisions of s. 7 will not automatically lead to exposure to the risk of a discovery assessment for up to 20 years. The rule concerns cases where the loss of tax is attributable to such a failure. Therefore, an individual who simply stays "beneath the radar" and thus avoids reporting his income can have a discovery assessment going back 20 years. However, an individual who notifies chargeability late and then sends in a return which later proves to be inadequate should not be subject to the 20-year time limit unless one of the other conditions in s. 36(1A) is met.

Furthermore, as demonstrated in *Hextall*, if the taxpayer can show a reasonable excuse for not notifying chargeability, s. 118(2) deems there to be no failure. Accordingly, in such cases, the extended time limits are disapplied. The tribunal considered that the phrase "reasonable excuse" should be interpreted as equivalent to "taking reasonable care".

Law: TMA 1970, s. 7, 8, 36(1A)(b), 118(2); ITA 2007, s. 30
Case: *Hextall v HMRC* [2023] UKFTT 390 (TC)

Failure to notify of DOTAS arrangements

The Disclosure of Tax Avoidance Scheme (DOTAS) provisions were introduced in FA 2004 in order to provide what is now HMRC with early notice of new inventive avoidance schemes, so that (if considered appropriate) legislative changes could be made promptly, thereby limiting any tax leakage.

However, the rules do not simply put a burden on the promoters of such schemes: they also require the participants to include a scheme reference number (as given by HMRC to the promoters upon notification) on their relevant tax return(s). The clear purpose of this is to ensure that the participants' tax returns can be easily selected for enquiry. (The case law (for example, *Corbally-Stourton*) shows that the process does not always work; but that is the theory.)

Conversely, a taxpayer who fails to disclose participation in a notifiable tax avoidance scheme is less likely to be identified for enquiry, especially given the increased automation of the process which determines which returns are subject to enquiry. It is for this reason that failure by a taxpayer to make the relevant disclosure on his or her tax return will expose the taxpayer to a discovery assessment for up to 20 years after the end of the relevant tax year.

The 20-year time limit will apply if the taxpayer fails to make the required disclosure in the following cases:

- where the promoter is outside the UK (and there is no UK-resident promoter), the taxpayer is obliged to notify HMRC of the scheme (unless an overseas promoter has already complied with the duty);
- where there is in fact no promoter, the taxpayer is obliged to notify HMRC of the scheme; or
- where the promoter has been given a scheme reference number and that number has been passed to the taxpayer, the taxpayer is required to include the number on relevant tax returns.

Of course, as the statute makes clear, there has to be a connection between the avoidance scheme and the loss of tax subsequently discovered. Failure to disclose participation in a notified scheme should not expose the taxpayer to a 20-year time limit more generally.

It should also be remembered that the 20-year time limit applies only in cases where the taxpayer has failed to make the relevant disclosure. Any failure by the promoter (for example to notify HMRC in the first place or to pass on the scheme reference number to the taxpayer) will not trigger the 20-year time limit (although the promoter is likely to be subject to heavy penalties).

See also **8.3.2** below in relation to years before 2009-10.

Law: TMA 1970, s. 36(1A)(c); FA 2004, s. 309, 310, 313

Failure to notify under POTAS

FA 2014 introduced rules to monitor certain promoters of tax avoidance schemes (POTAS). Under these rules, a monitored promoter is obliged to notify certain clients of the promoter's reference number which will be allocated as a consequence of being monitored. Furthermore, these clients will in some cases be obliged to pass the promoter's reference number to third parties.

If a person has been duly notified of a promoter reference number and that person expects to obtain a tax advantage from that promoter's arrangements, then a report must be made to HMRC, usually in a tax return. If the person fails to make the report, then a discovery assessment may be made up to 20 years after the end of the tax year so as to remedy any under-assessment attributable to those arrangements.

Law: TMA 1970, s. 36(1A)(d); FA 2014, s. 253

8.2.5   Deceased taxpayers

Assessments made before the taxpayer's death

In *Wood*, the Upper Tribunal noted that, on human rights grounds, HMRC should drop penalty assessments and determinations in circumstances where a taxpayer has since died.

However, the tribunal confirmed that pursuing an assessment made before the taxpayer's death under the 20-year extended time limits (because of deliberate conduct) did not breach the human rights of the deceased's personal representatives.

Case: *Personal Representative of Michael Wood (deceased) v HMRC* [2016] UKUT 346 (TCC)

Additional time limit on assessments

As noted above, if a taxpayer has died, assessments under s. 34, 35 or 36 must be made on the taxpayer's personal representatives within four years of the end of the tax year in which the death occurred.

Law: TMA 1970, s. 40(1)

Alternative time limit available to HMRC

However, an alternative time limit can also be invoked by HMRC in cases involving a loss of tax brought about carelessly or deliberately either by the deceased or by a person previously acting on the deceased's behalf (i.e. before the death occurred). In such cases, an assessment:

- may be made to cover a tax year ending up to six years before the taxpayer's death; but
- must be made within four years after the end of the tax year in which the taxpayer died.

Law: TMA 1970, s. 40(2)

8.3 Transitional rule

8.3.1 Introduction

The time limits were radically overhauled with effect from 1 April 2010, principally to make it harder for HMRC to issue discovery assessments (mainly by reducing the usual time limit from six years to four and the extended time limit in cases of carelessness down from twenty years to six). However, the rules did extend the time limits in cases of failures to notify chargeability and failures under DOTAS. (The POTAS rules were not then in force.)

As the new time limits apply by reference to the date on which the discovery assessment was made, transitional rules were introduced to ensure that the changes did not have the effect of retrospectively enabling HMRC to issue assessments in cases where, previously, no such right existed.

As noted at **5.2.2** above, however, the transitional rule delayed the onset of the new time limits until 1 April 2012 is very unlikely to have any practical effect.

Law: SI 2009/403, art. 2(2), 10

8.3.2 Failure to notify chargeability or DOTAS scheme participation

As noted at **8.2.4**, with effect from 1 April 2010, the provisions in s. 36(1A)(b) and (c) (respectively, failure to notify chargeability to tax and failure to notify participation in a DOTAS-notified scheme) give rise to the risk of discovery assessments for up to 20 years.

These provisions, however, cannot apply if:

- the tax year is the 2008-09 tax year (or earlier); and
- the loss of tax is not attributable to the taxpayer's negligent conduct or to the negligent conduct of a person acting on the taxpayer's behalf.

The reason for the second condition is that cases where there was such negligent conduct could (under the pre-2010 rules) be subject to a 20-year time limit in any event.

Law: SI 2009/403, art. 7

8.4 Modifications for offshore matters

8.4.1 Requirement to correct

Where the assessment seeks to rectify an under-assessment in relation to an offshore matter, HMRC could assess at any time until 5 April 2021 provided that:

- there was a matter to be corrected at the end of the 2016-17 tax year; and
- the time limit would otherwise have fallen between 6 April 2017 and 5 April 2021.

Law: F(No. 2)A 2017, Sch. 18, para. 26(1)

8.4.2 Extended time limits for offshore assessments

However, FA 2019 has since introduced a 12-year time limit for all assessments involving an offshore matter (including any offshore transfer which makes the lost tax significantly harder to identify).

However, this extension to the time limits will not apply if HMRC had received information from overseas authorities under mandatory automatic exchange provisions, which should reasonably have enabled HMRC to be aware of the lost tax and to have made an assessment before the ordinary time limits. Nor will it apply in relation to any additional tax arising from a transfer pricing adjustment.

This extension clearly has no effect in cases of deliberate under-assessment, where a 20-year limit already applies.

In cases of carelessness, however, the 12-year rule applies for 2013-14 and later tax years. In other cases, the 12-year rule applies only for 2015-16 and later years. There is therefore some overlap with the provisions considered at **8.4.1**.

Scott was a case involving the 2013-14 and 2014-15 tax years, in which HMRC accepted that there was no carelessness. Thus, s. 36A could not apply. However, that did not preclude the rule considered at **8.4.1** from applying.

Law: TMA 1970, s. 36A; FA 2019, s. 80
Case: *Scott v HMRC* [2023] UKFTT 360 (TC)

8.5   Other taxes

8.5.1   *Corporation tax*

Generally

As well as the time limits set out in the paragraphs that follow, there can be other instances where a longer time limit may be permitted under the statute. One example is in cases where a provisional claim for rollover relief has lapsed because no replacement asset has been purchased within the allowed period.

It should also be noted that time limits for corporation tax assessments run from the end of the accounting period to which the assessment relates.

Thus particular care should be taken in cases where a company changes accounting dates or if an accounting period has come to an end by virtue of a statutory rule (for example, a company ceasing to be within the charge to corporation tax).

Law: TCGA 1992, s. 153A(4)(b); CTA 2009, s. 10

The basic time limit

The basic time limit for corporation tax assessments is four years from the end of the accounting period to which the assessment relates.

Law: FA 1998, Sch. 18, para. 46(1)

Six-year time limit in cases of careless conduct

As with income tax and CGT, there is a two-year extension in cases of careless conduct, thereby requiring an assessment to be made within six years of the end of the accounting period to which it relates.

For this extension to be relevant, there has to be careless conduct by either the company or what the statute calls "a related person". This term is defined below.

Law: FA 1998, Sch. 18, para. 46(2)

20-year time limit in more serious cases

As with income tax and CGT, a 20-year time limit applies in more serious cases. For corporation tax purposes, HMRC must show that the loss of income tax or CGT is either:

- brought about deliberately by the company or a related person (as defined below);
- attributable to the company's failure to comply with an obligation to notify HMRC that it is chargeable to corporation tax for an accounting period within 12 months of the end of that accounting period (under FA 1998, Sch. 18, para. 2);
- (subject to the transitional rule at **8.3.2** above) attributable to arrangements in which the company has failed to comply with DOTAS notification obligations under FA 2004, s. 309, 310 or 313; or
- attributable to arrangements in which the company has failed to comply with a POTAS notification obligation under FA 2014, s. 253.

It will be noted that the latter three conditions do not turn on any failures by third parties – only failures by the company itself.

Law: FA 1998, Sch. 18, para. 46(2A); SI 2009/403, art. 8

Related person

For these purposes, a related person is either:

- a person acting on the company's behalf; or
- a person who was a partner of the company at the relevant date.

Law: FA 1998, Sch. 18, para. 46(2B)

8.5.2   SDLT

Change of time limits

Unlike the time limits for income tax, CGT and corporation tax, the time limits for SDLT discussed below changed with effect from 1 April 2011.

Law: SI 2010/867, art. 2(2)

The basic four-year time limit

SDLT also has a basic four-year time limit, by reference to the effective date of the transaction to which it relates. Thus, if the effective date of a transaction was 29 November 2021, there is no bar on any assessment being made on any date up to and including 29 November 2025.

Law: FA 2003, Sch. 10, para. 31(1)

Six-year time limit in cases of careless conduct

There is also a similar two-year extension in cases of careless conduct, thereby requiring an assessment to be made within six years of the effective date of the transaction to which it relates.

For this extension to be relevant, there has to be careless conduct either by the purchaser or by what the statute calls "a related person". This term is defined below.

This is subject to a further time limit in cases of taxpayers who have died (see below).

Law: FA 2003, Sch. 10, para. 31(2)

20-year time limit in more serious cases

There is similarly a 20-year time limit in more serious cases (subject to further time limits in cases where the purchaser has died – see below). For SDLT purposes, HMRC must show that the loss of tax is either:

- brought about deliberately by the purchaser or by a related person (as defined below);
- attributable to the purchaser's failure to comply with an obligation under any of the following provisions:
    - FA 2003, s. 76(1) (duty to deliver land transaction return); or
    - FA 2003, Sch. 17A, para. 3(3)(a), 4(3)(a) or 8(3)(a) (returns in cases involving leases);
- attributable to arrangements in which the purchaser has failed to comply with DOTAS notification obligations under FA 2004, s. 309, 310 or 313; or
- attributable to arrangements in which the purchaser has failed to comply with a POTAS notification obligation under FA 2014, s. 253.

It will be noted that the latter three conditions do not turn on any failures by third parties – only failures by the purchaser himself.

In the context of the second condition (a lack of return), the Court of Appeal in *Knight* considered similar legislation and concluded that two tests needed to be met: first, that there has been a lack of a return and, secondly, that the return (if filed) would have been filed correctly. But, it was subsequently decided in *Crest* that this two-stage process was not applicable in the context of self-assessed taxes (*Knight* predated self-assessment).

Perhaps due to oversight, there is no transitional provision limiting the extension of the time limits for DOTAS compliance failures.

Law: FA 2003, Sch. 10, para. 31(2A)

Cases: *Knight v IRC* (1974) 49 TC 179; *Crest Nicholson (Wainscott) v HMRC* [2017] UKFTT 134 (TC)

Related person

For these purposes, a related person is either:

- a person acting on the purchaser's behalf; or
- a person who was a partner of the purchaser at the relevant date.

Law: FA 2003, Sch. 10, para. 31(6)

Additional time limit in cases of deceased purchasers

In cases where the purchaser has died since the transaction, there is a further overriding restriction on the timing of any assessment to be made on the purchaser's personal representatives. That is that any assessment must be made within four years of the purchaser's death.

The legislation suggests that there is a further time limit of six years from the effective date of the transaction. However, that is stated to apply only to cases within para. 31(2) (careless conduct) which are already governed by a six-year time limit. The provision made more sense before 1 April 2011 when longer time limits were available to HMRC in cases of negligent and fraudulent conduct.

It is possible that this overriding six-year time limit (in cases of deceased purchasers) was also intended to remain in place in all cases governed by the 20-year time limit. However, it appears that the intention has not been properly implemented in the statute.

Law: FA 2003, Sch. 10, para. 31(4)

8.5.3   ATED

The basic four-year time limit

ATED also has a basic four-year time limit, by reference to the chargeable period to which it relates.

Law: FA 2013, Sch. 33, para. 25(1)

Six-year time limit in cases of careless conduct

There is also a similar two-year extension in cases of careless conduct, thereby requiring an assessment to be made within six years after the end of the chargeable period to which the assessment relates.

For this extension to be relevant, there has to be careless conduct either by the taxpayer or by what the statute calls "a related person". This term is defined below.

This is subject to a further time limit in cases of taxpayers who have died (see below).

Law: FA 2013, Sch. 33, para. 25(2)

20-year time limit in more serious cases

There is similarly a 20-year time limit in more serious cases (subject to further time limits in cases where the taxpayer has died – see below). For ATED purposes, HMRC must show that the loss of tax is either:

- brought about deliberately by the taxpayer or a related person (as defined below);
- attributable to the taxpayer's failure to comply with an obligation under FA 2013, s. 159(1) or 160(1) (duty to make ATED return or return of adjusted chargeable amount);
- attributable to arrangements in which the taxpayer has failed to comply with DOTAS notification obligations under FA 2004, s. 309, 310 or 313; or
- attributable to arrangements in which the taxpayer has failed to comply with a POTAS notification obligation under FA 2014, s. 253.

It will be noted that the latter three conditions do not turn on any failures by third parties – only failures by the taxpayer himself.

Law: FA 2013, Sch. 33, para. 25(3), (4)

Related person

For these purposes, a related person is either:

- a person acting on the taxpayer's behalf; or
- a person who was a partner of the taxpayer at the relevant date.

Law: FA 2013, Sch. 33, para. 25(9)

Additional time limit in cases of deceased taxpayers

In cases where the taxpayer has died, there is a further overriding restriction on the timing of any assessment to be made on the taxpayer's personal representatives. That is that any assessment must be made within four years of the taxpayer's death.

The legislation suggests that there is a further rule preventing assessments from being made in relation to chargeable periods ending more than six years before the taxpayer's death. However, that rule is stated to apply only to cases within para. 25(2) (careless conduct) which are already governed by a six-year time limit.

It is possible that this overriding six-year time limit (in cases of deceased purchasers) was also intended also to apply in cases governed by the 20-year time limit. However, it appears that the intention has not been properly implemented in the statute. One possible explanation is that the legislation has been modelled on the equivalent (and similarly faulty) rules relating to SDLT (see **8.5.2** above).

Law: FA 2013, Sch. 33, para. 25(7)

8.5.4   Digital services tax

For digital services tax, the normal four-year, six-year and 20-year time limits apply. In addition, there is a 20-year time limit where tax is lost "as a result of a failure by the responsible member to register with HMRC" when threshold conditions are met.

Law: FA 2020, Sch. 8, para. 21

8.5.5   Public interest business protection tax

For public interest business protection tax, the normal four-year, six-year and 20-year time limits apply.

Law: FA 2022, Sch. 10, para. 20

8.5.6   Multinational top-up tax

For multinational top-up tax, the normal four-year, six-year and 20-year time limits apply. In addition, there is a 20-year time limit where tax is lost "as a result of a failure of a filing member to register with HMRC".

Law: F(No. 2)A 2023, Sch. 14, para. 29

8.6   Other discovery provisions

8.6.1   Non-resident capital gains tax

The four-year time limit for income tax and CGT is expressly applied to cover non-resident CGT determinations, applicable for periods up to 5 April 2019.

Although there is no express power to allow non-resident CGT determinations after more than four years, HMRC can simply use their normal assessment powers under s. 29 to recover the CGT that they consider to be due. Therefore, HMRC do in fact in practice have the right to recover the tax after more than four years in cases involving careless or deliberate conduct.

Law: TMA 1970, s. 34(1A)

8.6.2   Partnership returns

There appears to be no time limit for discovery amendments to be made to partnership returns or any consequential amendments made on the partners.

Law: TMA 1970, s. 30B(1), (2)

9.   Procedural matters

9.1   HMRC procedures when an officer makes an assessment

9.1.1   Internal procedures

The legislation is silent as to any procedures that ought to be followed when a discovery assessment is made, and such matters are left for HMRC's own internal guidance.

One particular procedure worth noting is in cases where an assessment is made more than four years after the end of the tax year to which the assessment relates, what HMRC refer to as an "extended time limit assessment". In such cases, HMRC's guidance requires officers to obtain the authorisation of "the appropriate authorising officer".

Any failure to comply with such a duty, however, would not render the assessment invalid.

In *Kothari*, the FTT noted that it is usually unnecessary for the tribunal to be sure of the identity of the officer who finally made the decision to issue the assessment. This was also the approach taken in *Wilby*:

> "It is right that an officer must have made the discovery. However, I do not agree that it is inevitably the case that the assessment is not valid if the officer cannot be identified within the appeal. This is because the legislation does not say that the officer needs to be named. If a Tribunal can be satisfied that an officer has taken the decision then the decision is one by an appropriate individual person rather than based on any impermissible collective knowledge or collective conduct."

The FTT was comforted by the fact that the assessment "procedure was a tightly controlled one and that there is nothing to suggest that it was not followed as a matter of course".

Nevertheless, this is not to mean that taxpayers should not check that internal procedures have been carried out. HMRC must still demonstrate that a discovery has been made. As the FTT continued in *Wilby*:

"HMRC needs to establish what the subjective belief of the officer was when making the decision to assess and that this is necessarily difficult if the officer cannot be identified. However, this is an evidential matter for the Tribunal on the balance of probabilities. It might be a rare case in which this can be made out in the absence of evidence from the officer in question, but this does not mean that it can never be made out."

Cases: *Kothari v HMRC* [2019] UKFTT 423 (TC); *Wilby v HMRC* [2022] UKFTT 348 (TC)
Guidance: CH 53300

9.1.2   External procedures

In most cases, a discovery assessment will be valid only if an additional statutory condition is met (see **4.1** above). In practice, HMRC will usually explain on the face of the assessment (or in any letter issued at the same time) which condition(s) they consider to be satisfied. Furthermore, this would represent good practice so that a taxpayer is clearly made aware of the additional potential grounds of challenge.

However, there is no statutory obligation for this to take place and, therefore, a discovery assessment cannot be challenged on the basis that the additional statutory hurdle has not been expressly specified.

In *Hankinson*, the Court of Appeal went further and concluded that the officer need not even consider whether the additional conditions for a discovery assessment are met; instead, these conditions need not be considered until such time as the discovery assessment is challenged on appeal. On the other hand, it would be rather reckless for an officer to proceed with an assessment without believing that the assessment would be upheld on appeal. As a result, the practical consequence of the *Hankinson* judgment is in most cases simply that an officer might consider (say) the test in s. 29(4) to be satisfied, but it might subsequently transpire that a court or tribunal considers s. 29(5) to be satisfied instead.

Case: *Hankinson v HMRC* [2011] EWCA Civ 1566

9.1.3   Statutory provisions

The statute provides that a single assessment may cover more than one type of income.

So far as obligations on HMRC are concerned, the only practical statutory requirements for an assessment are that:

- notice of the assessment shall be served on the person assessed; and
- the notice shall state both the date of issue and the time within which any appeal against the assessment may be made.

The practical consequence of the former requirement is that HMRC may not simply serve notice on the taxpayer's agent although, in practice, they will usually issue the agent with a copy under the form 64-8 procedures.

Notices of assessment may be delivered or left at the taxpayer's usual or last known place of residence. Notices may also be served by post. Although typically sent to taxpayers' home addresses, the legislation also permits service at the taxpayer's place of business or employment.

In *Tinkler*, the Court of Appeal held that statutory notices cannot routinely be served on taxpayers' agents. This is consistent with long-established HMRC practice requiring such notices to be served on the taxpayer. This aspect of the court's decision was not disputed when the case proceeded to the Supreme Court.

In *Astar*, the tribunal considered the validity of an assessment sent to the wrong address. The implication of the tribunal's decision is that improper service could invalidate the assessment but it would depend on whether the person serving the document could "have any reasonable basis to believe that the [intended recipient] resided at the address". As the taxpayer had itself cited the (albeit) wrong address, it was held not to be unreasonable for HMRC to have served the assessment there.

Law: TMA 1970, s. 30A(2), (3), 115(1), (2)

Cases: *Astar Services Ltd v HMRC* [2018] UKFTT 463 (TC); *Tinkler v HMRC* [2019] EWCA Civ 1392

Assessments on trustees and personal representatives

In cases of trustees and personal representatives (being situations where there are usually two or more persons who are acting in such a capacity), the assessment may be issued in the name of a single trustee or personal representative.

Law: TMA 1970, s. 30AA

9.1.4   Inadequate notice

Given that the statute distinguishes between assessments and notices of assessment, the latter being the means by which a taxpayer is informed of the fact of an assessment, the critical date for the purposes of time limits is the date on which the assessment is made, and not when it is notified to the taxpayer. This was at the heart of the dispute in *Honig v Sarsfield* (see **8.1.2** above).

On the other hand, it is not sufficient for an assessment to be made (within the time limit), only for notice to be sent out at some significantly later stage. In *Kothari*, the FTT stated as follows:

> "While it is clear that the legislation draws a distinction between the making and notification of an assessment, and there is no requirement for the notice of assessment to be issued by the final deadline for an assessment being made, nevertheless both steps are part of a single assessing procedure so there must be some proximity or nexus between the two steps."

Cases: *Honig v Sarsfield (HM Inspector of Taxes)* [1986] STC 246, [1986] BTC 205; *Kothari v HMRC* [2019] UKFTT 423 (TC)

What constitutes notice

There is very little guidance as to what constitutes valid notice to the taxpayer. This is unsurprising given the lack of statutory requirements in this regard.

In *Hallamshire*, the High Court made it clear that to be valid a notice of assessment had to enable the taxpayer to be "told what tax he has to pay, not merely given the information from which a skilled adviser would be able to decide the tax eventually to be demanded".

Furthermore, in the light of the *Tinkler* case, it is clear that notices of assessment should be given to the taxpayer (or at least sent to the taxpayer's last-known residence).

In the context of VAT, in *Queenspice*, the Upper Tribunal approved the following guidance as to the ingredients of a valid notice:

"In judging the validity of notification, the test is whether the relevant documents contain between them, in unambiguous and reasonably clear terms, a notification to the taxpayer containing (a) the taxpayer's name, (b) the amount of tax due, (c) the reason for the assessment, and (d) the period of time to which it relates."

Cases: *Hallamshire Industrial Finance Trust Limited v CIR* (1978) 53 TC 631; *Queenspice Ltd v HMRC* [2011] UKUT 11; *Tinkler v HMRC* [2019] EWCA Civ 1392

9.2 Taxpayer procedures following an assessment

9.2.1 Payment of tax

The amount of tax charged by an assessment is a debt payable to HMRC. The date on which it is payable (i.e. the date from which HMRC may commence enforcement proceedings) depends on the date on which the taxpayer is "given" notice of the assessment, rather than the date on which notice of the assessment is issued.

The word "given" was examined by the Special Commissioner in *Holly* in the context of the receipt of enquiry notices. If the notice is given on day 1, the tax is due on day 30.

Under the *Interpretation Act*, if a document is posted and properly addressed with postage properly paid, it is generally deemed to have been given on the day on which it would arrived "in the ordinary course of post". However, this presumption is rebuttable if there is evidence of delivery on a different date (or of non-delivery).

This is subject to the taxpayer's right to postpone the tax payable (see **9.2.3** below). In all cases, though, interest will run from the original due date of the tax, which will usually be the date on which the tax would have been payable had it been properly included in the taxpayer's return for the period in question.

Law: TMA 1970, s. 59B(6); *Interpretation Act* 1978, s. 7
Case: *Holly & Anor v HM Inspector of Taxes* (1999) Sp C 225

9.2.2 Appealing to HMRC

There is almost always a statutory right of appeal against a discovery assessment. The only theoretical exception is where there is a statutory provision that provides that one type of assessment is conclusive in appeal against another type of assessment.

An appeal must be made in writing, within 30 days of the date of issue of the notice of assessment, to the officer who issued the notice.

The notice of appeal must state the grounds of appeal.

Law: TMA 1970, s. 31, 31A

Subject matter of an appeal

The grounds of appeal may cover either or both of:

- the subject matter of the assessment (often described as the substantive issue);
- the necessary components for discovery assessments (often described as a procedural challenge).

Furthermore, the statute specifically provides that any challenge to the validity of an assessment based on the conditions referred to in **4.1** above must be made by way of appeal against the assessment. In other words, a taxpayer may not use the invalidity of a discovery assessment as a defence against enforcement proceedings or against a penalty for late payment of the tax. Nor should judicial review proceedings be used for any such challenge.

Strictly speaking, this obligation to make a challenge by way of appeal does not apply to cases where the argument is that there has been no discovery (see **Chapter 3**). There is theoretically the risk, therefore, that the tribunal could decide that it does not have jurisdiction to hear such challenges and that any such argument ought to have been made by way of judicial review. In practice, however, the tribunal (as did its statutory predecessors) has entertained arguments about the non-fulfilment of the fundamental obligation for there to be a discovery and it is not expected that it will relinquish this assumed jurisdiction in the future.

Furthermore, one could raise the argument that the discovery assessment is valid only if there has been a prior discovery and the tribunal has jurisdiction to hear an appeal against an assessment only if the assessment is itself valid. Therefore, any challenge along the grounds that there has been no discovery is effectively an argument concerning the tribunal's jurisdiction and, as held in *Jacques*, the tribunal always has jurisdiction to consider whether or not it has jurisdiction.

In any event, the previous blanket rule against the FTT entertaining arguments that would more traditionally be considered in the course of a judicial review has been somewhat diluted. For example, in *Birkett*, the Upper Tribunal made clear that public law arguments may be made in the FTT "in the course of exercising the jurisdiction which it does have". Thus, if a taxpayer challenges an assessment by way of appeal to the FTT then the FTT has the right to consider the procedural validity of the assessment.

Law: TMA 1970, s. 29(8)

Cases: *B W Jacques v HMRC* (2005) Sp C 513; *R & J Birkett t/a The Orchards Residential Home v HMRC* [2017] UKUT 89 (TCC)

9.2.3   Postponement of tax

Even if an appeal is made against a discovery assessment, the default position is that the tax remains payable and can be the subject of enforcement proceedings.

However, in cases where there is an appeal against the assessment, the taxpayer has the right to seek a postponement (i.e. HMRC's agreement not to enforce payment) pending resolution of the appeal.

To exercise this right, a written request has to be made within 30 days of the date on which the notice of assessment is issued, stating the reasons for believing the assessment to be excessive. In practice, the postponement application will usually be made at the same time as the appeal itself is made to HMRC.

HMRC will almost invariably agree to such applications but, if not, the matter can be referred to the tribunal.

A postponement application may also be made more than 30 days after the issue of the notice of assessment. However, strictly speaking, postponement is then available only if there is a change in the circumstances.

The right to postpone the payment of tax is removed in cases where the taxpayer has also received an accelerated payment notice (APN) or a partner payment notice (PPN). In cases where the APN or PPN arrives after postponement has already been given, the postponement will cease to be effective once the APN or PPN becomes final and fully effective (i.e. after 90 days, or 30 days after rejection of representations if later).

Law: TMA 1970, s. 55

9.3   Burden of proof

9.3.1   Generally

If matters are not resolved at an earlier stage, the case will progress to the FTT. The procedures at, and in the lead-up to, any such hearing should follow the legal question as to which party has the burden of proof.

It is generally well understood that taxpayers have the burden of proof at appeals. However, this is somewhat an over-simplification as the burden can differ in relation to different aspects of an appeal.

9.3.2   Substantive matter

If HMRC have assessed a taxpayer for a sum of money, then the burden is on the taxpayer to show that the assessment is seeking an excessive amount (either that the amount stated is too high or that the assessment is wrong in principle – or both).

The statutory justification for this is TMA 1970, s. 50(6) which reads:

> "If, on an appeal notified to the tribunal, the tribunal decides–
>
> ...
>
> (c) that the appellant is overcharged by an assessment other than a self-assessment,
>
> the assessment or amounts shall be reduced accordingly, but otherwise the assessment or statement shall stand good."

The theory is that the assessment is deemed to be right unless one party (and it will typically be the taxpayer) is able to persuade the tribunal that the amount should be reduced. Such persuasion will be based upon law and/or fact, with facts proved on the balance of probability.

(For completeness, one should not overlook the corresponding provisions of s. 50(7), which permit the tribunal to *increase* the amount of an assessment. Again, evidence will be needed to justify any such increase.)

The point was made particularly clear in *Nicholson* where it was emphasised that an assessment might well be for the wrong amount but it stands until such time as there is evidence to show not just that it is incorrect but also what the correct amount is:

> "Even supposing that I were myself to think that the amounts were wrong – and, as I have freely conceded, and as [Counsel for the Revenue] has freely conceded, they probably are wrong – what on earth could I or anybody else at this stage, in the total absence of evidence, substitute for them? The answer is that it is a complete and utter impossibility; and that is why, of course, the *Taxes Management Act* throws upon the taxpayer the onus of showing that the assessments are wrong. It is the taxpayer who knows and the taxpayer who is in a position (or, if not in a position, who certainly should be in a position) to provide the right answer, and chapter and verse for the right answer, and it is idle for any taxpayer to say to the Revenue, 'Hidden somewhere in your vaults are the right answers: go thou and dig them out of the vaults.' That is not a duty on the Revenue. If it were, it would be a very onerous, very costly and very expensive operation, the costs of which would of course fall entirely on the taxpayers as a body. It is the duty of every individual taxpayer to make his own return and, if challenged, to support the return he has made, or, if that return cannot be supported, to come completely clean, and if he gives no evidence whatsoever he cannot be surprised if he is finally lumbered with more than he has in fact received. It is his own fault that he is so lumbered."

Ultimately, the principle of requiring the taxpayer to disprove the assessment is a question of policy. As similarly held by the Privy Council in *Bi-Flex*:

"The element of guess-work and the almost unavoidable inaccuracy in a properly made best of judgment assessment, as the cases have established, do not serve to displace the validity of the assessments, which are *prima facie* right and remain right until the taxpayer shows that they are wrong and also shows positively what corrections should be made in order to make the assessments right or more nearly right. It is also relevant, when considering the sufficiency of evidence to displace an assessment, to remember that the facts are peculiarly within the knowledge of the taxpayer."

It was clear in the High Court in *Johnson*, that in many cases it will be necessary for the officer to draw inferences when determining how much to assess. Nevertheless, this does not permit HMRC to make wild and speculative assessments simply in order to require a taxpayer to engage in the process and reduce the assessment. As the Court of Appeal agreed in *Johnson*:

"The fact that the onus is on the taxpayer to displace the assessment is not intended to give the Crown *carte blanche* to make wild or extravagant claims. Where an inference of whatever nature falls to be made, one invariably speaks of a 'fair' inference."

This approach led to one pair of assessments being vacated by the FTT in *Ritchie*.

Similarly, the VAT case-law typified in *Rahman* says that "an honest and genuine attempt to make a reasoned assessment" should suffice. However, if the amount cannot be reasonably explained, "the proper inference may be that the assessment was indeed arbitrary".

Accordingly, in *Cussens*, the tribunal allowed a taxpayer's appeals because there was no evidence "to suggest that any thought, consideration or analysis whatsoever" had been undertaken before HMRC made their assessments and that the amounts assessed represented figures "plucked from the air".

McCloskey concerned a question of whether the asserted under-assessment arose from deliberate conduct, something that HMRC are required to prove (see **9.3.3**). In that case, the tribunal noted that HMRC cannot discharge the burden simply by making a "best judgment" assessment as to what they consider to be the correct amount of tax. Similar principles should apply in the context of careless conduct.

Law: TMA 1970, s. 50(6), (7)

Cases: *Nicholson v Morris (HM Inspector of Taxes)* (1976) 51 TC 95; *Bi-Flex Caribbean Ltd v Board of Inland Revenue* (1990) 63 TC 515; *Johnson v Scott (HM Inspector of Taxes)* (1978) 52 TC 383; *Rahman v HM Customs & Excise (No. 2)* [2002] EWCA Civ 1881; *Ritchie & Ritchie v HMRC* [2017] UKFTT 449 (TC); *McCloskey v HMRC* [2018] UKFTT 352 (TC); *Cussens v HMRC* [2019] UKFTT 543 (TC)

Domicile cases

There is potentially a different approach to be taken in domicile cases because of a principle in such cases (not specific to tax matters) that any party arguing for a change of domicile bears the burden of proof, as made clear in the case of *Cyganik*. In tax cases, that party might well be the taxpayer (seeking to show the acquisition of an overseas domicile of choice) but could equally be HMRC seeking to argue that a taxpayer has become domiciled in one of the constituent parts of the UK.

Domicile cases in the tribunal were exceedingly rare. Nevertheless, a recent campaign by HMRC to challenge taxpayers' claims to be domiciled overseas, which has led to a spate of cases dealing with a range of different procedural questions, has caused this issue to become live.

The approach taken so far (with which the author concurs) is that:

- as the starting point, the taxpayer will bear the burden of proof to displace an assessment; but
- (in a case where HMRC are arguing for change of domicile) the taxpayer's burden will generally be discharged by any common ground as to the taxpayer's domicile prior to the alleged change.

This is perhaps best illustrated with an example.

Example

Agnes, who was born in New Zealand, has been living in London for 20 years and HMRC now assert that she is domiciled in England and Wales. They accordingly assess her in respect of her unremitted income.

If it is common ground that Agnes has a domicile of origin (or was otherwise previously domiciled) outside the UK then the burden of proof will shift to HMRC to demonstrate that Agnes has indeed acquired a UK domicile.

However, if there is no common ground as to Agnes's domicile at any earlier date, then Agnes will first need to demonstrate that she has at some point had an overseas domicile, so that HMRC will be obliged to demonstrate a subsequent acquisition of UK domicile.

Case: *Cyganik v Agulian* [2006] EWCA Civ 129

9.3.3   Discovery assessments

With discovery cases, it is now firmly understood that the burden of proof lies on HMRC to demonstrate that the relevant procedural conditions for a discovery assessment are met.

This means that HMRC must demonstrate:

- that an officer has made the requisite discovery;
- if a return had been made, that at least one of the two additional conditions for a discovery assessment is met; and
- if relevant and not already covered by the previous point, that any time limits have been validly extended.

In one case (*County*), a Special Commissioner considered that the rule in TMA s. 29(8) (requiring challenges on the basis of non-fulfilment of the additional conditions required for a discovery assessment to be made by way of appeal) meant that the burden of proof in relation to such matters fell on taxpayers in precisely the same way as it does in relation to the substantive matter of an appeal.

However, this was disapproved of in *Sanderson* where the judge followed the *obiter* guidance in *Household*.

Since then, it appears to have been fully accepted by HMRC that they have the burden of proof in showing that all the procedural ingredients for a discovery assessment are met.

For example, in *Kingdon*, the case ultimately turned on a binary question being whether a partnership transferred its trade to a company on one date (as suggested by HMRC) or an earlier date (as argued for by the taxpayers). It was common ground (a view that was also endorsed by the tribunal) that, to justify HMRC's discovery assessment, HMRC had to prove that their preferred date was correct.

Finally, it should be noted that F(No. 2)A 2017 reversed the burden of proof when it comes to questions of carelessness in tax avoidance cases. However, that provision applies solely in the context of penalties. For discovery assessments, therefore, it remains the case that it is for HMRC to prove any carelessness alleged.

Law: TMA 1970, s. 29(8); FA 2007, Sch. 24, para. 3A(2)

Cases: *County Pharmacy Ltd v HMRC* (2005) Sp C 495; *HMRC v Household Estate Agents Ltd* [2007] EWHC 1684 (Ch); *Sanderson v HMRC* [2012] UKFTT 207 (TC); *Kingdon v HMRC* [2022] UKFTT 407 (TC)

Cases of alleged carelessness or deliberate conduct

The fact that it is for HMRC to prove any careless or deliberate conduct was clearly implicit in the first strand of the *Hargreaves* litigation which concluded in 2016 with the (now) final decision of the Court of Appeal.

In the second strand of that litigation, Mr Hargreaves sought to challenge the First-tier's conclusion that he had completed his tax return negligently (being the test applicable in that case). In the Upper Tribunal, it was held that HMRC had put forward *prima facie* evidence of negligence (by demonstrating that Mr Hargreaves ought to have sought further professional advice about his residence status), which Mr Hargreaves could have displaced (for example, with evidence as to having in fact sought such further advice or with reasons as to why such further advice was considered unnecessary). However, as the Upper Tribunal continued, "when Mr Hargreaves chose to put forward no evidence at all to answer the *prima facie* case, the FTT was entitled to conclude that he had indeed breached his duty".

This principle underlying where the burden lies can also be seen in *Munford*. In that case, a taxpayer had claimed main residence exemption on a property, which he and his family had occupied for a matter of only a few weeks, without any significant moving of the family's furniture. Although those facts would be strong pointers towards the property not constituting a residence, they were held to be insufficient to constitute evidence that an erroneous claim to relief had been made deliberately.

It should be noted that in *Atherton*, however, the tribunal considered that HMRC can discharge the burden of proof in cases alleging carelessness simply by identifying an error in the tax return. If that is correct, taxpayers are required to show that they have taken reasonable care to avoid any under-assessment. In the author's respectful opinion, the tribunal's view in *Atherton* subverts the concept of the burden of proof and should not be followed. However, the Upper Tribunal (albeit *obiter*) appears to have upheld the FTT's view on this matter on the facts of the case.

Cases: *Hargreaves v HMRC* [2016] EWCA Civ 174; *Munford v HMRC* [2017] UKFTT 19 (TC); *Atherton v HMRC* [2017] UKFTT 831 (TC); *Atherton v HMRC* [2019] UKUT 41 (TCC); *Hargreaves v HMRC* [2022] UKUT 34 (TCC)

Cases of alleged insufficiency of disclosure

In respect of cases that turn on the information said to be before the hypothetical officer, the tribunal suggested the following in *Carter*:

- the burden of proof ordinarily falls on HMRC; but
- if HMRC have made out a prima facie case that the document containing the information in question was not sent to them, and so the information would not be attributable to the hypothetical officer, it is for the taxpayer to prove that the document was in fact so sent.

Case: *Carter & Kennedy v HMRC* [2020] UKFTT 179 (TC)

Burden of proof when arguing prevailing practice

There is, however, one aspect of the discovery assessment procedural provisions where the taxpayer has the burden of proof. This is in the relatively rare situation where a taxpayer seeks to argue that an assessment should be declared invalid because the original return was made on the basis or in accordance with the practice generally prevailing at the time when it was made (see **7.2** above).

Absence of evidence and adverse inferences

In many cases, an individual will not give evidence to explain his or her conduct or, having put forward evidence, the individual chooses not to attend and be subjected to cross-examination. In such cases, HMRC will often argue that an "adverse inference" should be drawn from the individual's reluctance.

Although there are situations in which an adverse inference can be properly drawn, it is not automatic and, in particular, no adverse inference is appropriate if the individual's absence can be explained. Furthermore, the possibility of the tribunal drawing an adverse inference does not overcome the other side's need to put forward a *prima facie* case. As the Upper Tribunal made clear in *Hargreaves*:

> "That said, the significance of Mr Hargreaves' decision not to give evidence is limited. It justified the FTT's conclusion that a breach of duty was established, but did not give rise to any special inference that all elements of HMRC's accusation of negligence were established. Specifically, it did not necessarily establish that the Situation was "attributable to" Mr Hargreaves' breach of duty."

Case: *Hargreaves v HMRC* [2022] UKUT 34 (TCC)

9.4   Practical consequences of where burden of proof falls

9.4.1   *The need to satisfy the burden of proof*

Although not universally true, it is the case that HMRC sometimes fail to alert taxpayers to the fact that the validity of their discovery assessment is dependent on certain statutory conditions being fulfilled. It is not clear whether this silence is due to the officer's own ignorance or oversight or whether it is in the hope that the taxpayer is unaware of the challenges that could be made.

As noted at **2.2.3** and **7.1** above, the Upper Tribunal in *Brimheath* concluded that HMRC are required to prove that each statutory component of a discovery assessment is satisfied unless the point has been expressly conceded by the taxpayer.

An example of this approach in practice can be seen in the case of *Norman*, where the tribunal noted:

> "We were not addressed by either representative on the fundamental point in s 29(1) TMA: was there a discovery? This was no doubt on Mr Oborne's [HMRC's presenting officer] part because he considered it obviously in his favour. But if there is no discovery the s 29 assessment cannot be a valid assessment."

Nevertheless, the author considers it would be prudent for taxpayers to make it clear in their notices of appeal that they require HMRC to prove that the conditions in s. 29 are met (again, except those conditions which are expressly conceded). The reason for this caution is that the Upper Tribunal (or a higher court) might subsequently qualify what was said in *Burgess/Brimheath* and decide that fairness dictates that HMRC must be put on proper notice as to what matters are in dispute.

Indeed, in the context of penalty appeals, in *Rogers*, the Upper Tribunal allowed an appeal by HMRC on the basis that they had not been given adequate notice of all the matters that they were required to prove. The two cases can be reconciled or at least distinguished. However, it is usually better to take a more cautious approach if given the chance and expressly identify each procedural point that is being taken.

Cases: *Norman v HMRC* [2015] UKFTT 303 (TC); *Burgess v HMRC, Brimheath Developments Ltd v HMRC* [2015] UKUT 578 (TCC); *HMRC v Rogers* [2019] UKUT 406 (TCC)

9.4.2   What needs to be proven and when?

The strict approach that a tribunal should take is to consider the following matters in the following order:

- first, whether the conditions for a discovery assessment are met (burden of proof on HMRC); and
- only then, whether the taxpayer is overcharged by the assessment (burden of proof on taxpayer);
- if there is no such overcharge then the taxpayer has the right to argue that the return was made in accordance with the prevailing practice (again, burden of proof on taxpayer).

The order of the first two legs was made clear by the Court of Appeal in *Hargreaves.* As the court held:

> "Even though the appeal raises other issues, Mr Hargreaves could at the end of HMRC's case, if HMRC open, submit that there was no case to answer on the conduct/officer condition [i.e. those in s. 29(4) and (5)]. If he won on that, there would be no valid DA. If he lost on that, he could then call his evidence on the substantive issues in his appeal, including section 29(2)."

It should be noted, however, that in the subsequent case of *Anderson*, the FTT expressly refused to hear a submission that there was no case to answer after hearing HMRC's evidence, notwithstanding the clear and binding words of the Court of Appeal:

> "The Appellant suggested that he had a right to have a decision on the preliminary issue before the tribunal continued to hear the substantive appeal. We do not agree. Other than the references in *Hargreaves*, we are not clear what 'right' the Appellant was asserting."

Cases: *Hargreaves v HMRC* [2016] EWCA Civ 174; *Anderson v HMRC* [2016] UKFTT 565 (TC)

9.4.3   Who goes first?

The above extract from *Hargreaves* makes it clear that the procedures to be followed depend also on the order of play at the tribunal hearing.

Ordinarily, taxpayers are expected to put their evidence first and to make their submissions ahead of HMRC simply because taxpayers bear the burden of proof. Nevertheless, it should be noted that the inherent flexibility of tribunal proceedings means that this normal pattern is not always followed.

In any event, in the context of discovery assessments, the burden of proof will fall on different parties in relation to different aspects of the case.

Hurley makes it clear that a taxpayer can require HMRC to go first and this is clearly consistent with what was later said in *Hargreaves*. Indeed, in *Hurley*, the Judge referred to *Amis* which goes so far as to suggest that HMRC are obliged to present their evidence first.

The author respectfully considers that the correct position is that (in discovery assessment cases) a taxpayer should always have the right to make HMRC present their evidence first. Furthermore, to the extent that HMRC wish to go first, the tribunal should similarly be expected to accede to such a request.

In such cases, *Amis* and *Hargreaves* explain the alternative courses of action available to HMRC. Either:

- HMRC should present all their evidence for the case; or
- HMRC should initially present only their evidence that justifies the making of a discovery assessment. Any further evidence is presented only once the tribunal has concluded that the assessment is procedurally valid.

Cases: *Amis v Colls (HM Inspector of Taxes)* (1960) 39 TC 148; *Hurley v Taylor (HM Inspector of Taxes)* [1998] STC 202, [1998] BTC 32; *Hargreaves v HMRC* [2016] EWCA Civ 174

9.4.4   Separate hearings

As noted above, HMRC need to prove the validity of the discovery assessment before the burden of proof falls on the taxpayer. There is therefore an argument that the validity of the discovery assessment should be dealt with at a preliminary hearing, so as to avoid the need for (what can often be) a complex hearing on the substantive issues.

As the *Hargreaves* case demonstrates, however, the taxpayer has no intrinsic right. Instead, the appropriateness of such a course of action is ultimately a matter for the tribunal, which has to consider whether a preliminary hearing is in the interests of justice. There is established case law (most notably in *Wrottesley*) which determines the factors that ought to be considered by a tribunal when an application is made for a separate preliminary hearing.

In *Hankinson*, it was considered that having a preliminary hearing was not appropriate. However, that was a case where HMRC were relying on alleged negligence (the fore-runner of careless conduct) and, as the Special Commissioner noted, "the issue of whether or not Mr Hankinson was negligent in treating himself as non-resident and not ordinarily resident for the purposes of the self-assessment return will depend on same sub-stratum of facts as will be relevant to the issue of whether he was in fact neither resident nor ordinarily resident". Because of this clear overlap of facts relating to both the procedural and substantive issues, the Special Commissioner considered that there should be a single hearing.

It is thought that the appropriateness of a single hearing is more acute in cases turning on either s. 29(1) itself (existence of a discovery) or s. 29(5) (quality of information available to the hypothetical officer), because neither of those issues turns on the actual facts of the taxpayer's substantive case. The attractiveness of a preliminary hearing to deal with the validity of a discovery assessment is particularly high in cases where the substantive issue would be relatively complex and there would therefore be considerable savings in time and cost if the assessment can be shown to be invalid at an early stage. This was acknowledged by the tribunal in *Addo* which noted that there will be some cases in which points on s. 29(5) can be taken without referring to the full details of the particular case (thereby permitting a preliminary hearing). However, it concluded that that was not such a case.

Nevertheless, in practice, it is not always possible to persuade the tribunal to take this course of action, as shown by the *Anderson* and *Addo* cases.

One rare exception was the case of *Milligan*, where the tribunal permitted the question as to the essential newness of a discovery assessment to be considered as a preliminary matter (that being before the Supreme Court dismissed the relevance of the issue). There is no explanation as to how the decision was taken to take discovery as a preliminary issue. However, the outcome is consistent with the detailed analysis in *Arunvill*. That too concerned an application for staleness to be carved out and considered at a preliminary hearing and the tribunal might well have acceded to that request. However, the tribunal was similarly aware that HMRC would be likely to challenge any finding of staleness by way of further appeal. When weighing up the factors in accordance with the *Wrottesley* approach, that led to the tribunal declining to grant the application.

However, a different view was expressed in *Mehrban*, where the decision published also turned on the validity of the discovery assessments. Even though the tribunal was aware that HMRC would be likely to appeal against its decision in relation to staleness, the tribunal noted that "much time, energy and expense could have been saved if the 'discovery issue' had been dealt with as a preliminary issue".

Cases: *Hankinson v R & C Commrs* (2007) Sp C 649; *Anderson v HMRC* [2009] UKFTT 258 (TC); *Wrottesley v HMRC* [2014] UKFTT 972 (TC); *Hargreaves v HMRC* [2016] EWCA Civ 174; *Addo v HMRC* [2016] UKFTT 787 (TC); *Milligan v HMRC* [2017] UKFTT 552 (TC); *Arunvill Global Equity Trading Ltd v HMRC* [2018] UKFTT 378 (TC); *Mehrban v HMRC* [2021] UKFTT 53 (TC)

9.5   Multiple errors

9.5.1   Introduction

It is inevitable that there will be cases in which a taxpayer's self-assessment will contain more than one error, each with a different cause and, more importantly, a different level of culpability.

Extra care needs to be taken in such cases to ensure that a discovery assessment does not go too far.

9.5.2   The historical approach

Historically, the approach was as typified in *Hudson*. There, it was held that once it has been shown that there had been (what is now) careless or deliberate conduct leading to an under-assessment, then HMRC are entitled to assess so as to correct all errors previously made by the taxpayer in relation to that tax year.

Case: *Hudson v Humbles (HM Inspector of Taxes)* (1965) 42 TC 380

9.5.3   A more modern approach

More recently, however, in *Bubb*, the tribunal took a more piecemeal approach. There, a taxpayer had made three distinct errors on his tax return, but only one of which was held to be careless. As it happens, however, HMRC's assessment had been made specifically to correct the *other* two errors. The tribunal concluded that, the proven carelessness notwithstanding, the appeal had to be allowed as the assessment actually made had not corrected any error attributable to the taxpayer's careless conduct.

The subsequent case of *Marsh* makes a similar point in relation to the concept of a discovery under s. 29(1). Having considered that there was carelessness due to the omission of property income, the tribunal continued:

> "But this small amount does not we think act as a peg, or jumping off point, to justify the much larger CGT assessment. We think that s 29(1) TMA must be considered separately in relation to each source at least as far as income and chargeable gains are concerned."

The point was reiterated in *Clark* when the tribunal held:

> "... an appeal against a discovery assessment does not open a general roving enquiry into the tax position of the appellant."

Consequently, where two different losses have been identified, the tribunal in *Clark* confirmed it is necessary to identify separately whether each loss satisfies the requirements of discovery in s. 29(1).

The Upper Tribunal subsequently upheld the conclusions in *Clark*. However, although it is considered that the logic adopted by the FTT is not to be faulted, the Upper Tribunal did not expressly comment on each aspect of the FTT's decision.

Cases: *Bubb v HMRC* [2016] UKFTT 216 (TC); *Marsh v HMRC* [2017] UKFTT 320 (TC); *Clark v HMRC* [2017] UKFTT 392 (TC); *Clark v HMRC* [2018] UKUT 397 (TCC)

9.5.4   *Reconciling the two approaches*

The two different approaches are in any event entirely reconcilable and the author is currently of the view that they can both be right.

Essentially, there must be a discovery in relation to each component of the assessment. Even if this can be shown, if HMRC are also to show that a discovery assessment is valid (see **Chapter 4**), they will still need to demonstrate that the relevant condition (s. 29(4) or (5)) is satisfied in relation to the subject-matter of the assessment. Thus, they will need to show either that:

- the assessment is rectifying an error attributable to careless or deliberate conduct of the taxpayer or a person acting on the taxpayer's behalf; or

- the error corrected could not have been identified by the hypothetical officer.

However, if the question is simply one of time limits, then all that is needed to be shown is the fact that there was some careless or deliberate conduct being rectified by the assessment so as to permit a full correction to be made.

It should be noted, however, that the rules for the validity of discovery assessments and those for time limits overlap. In particular, HMRC will often rely upon the same arguments to show both that they are entitled to make an assessment and that the assessment is not being made out of time. In such cases, the decision in *Bubb* should prevail.

Furthermore, the facts of *Bubb* were unusual and it is more likely that a discovery assessment will be made correcting *all* errors. It is the author's view, however, that the *Bubb* approach should still be adopted and will permit a discovery assessment only to the extent that each error corrected separately satisfies the relevant statutory conditions.

Nevertheless, it must be remembered that there are still cases in which the taxpayer did not make a tax return and therefore cannot require HMRC to overcome the hurdles discussed in **Chapters 5** and **6** above. In such cases, HMRC have a wider power to recover tax after four years.

Case: *Bubb v HMRC* [2016] UKFTT 216 (TC)

9.6   Appeals from the First-tier Tribunal

9.6.1   Introduction

It is firmly established that an appeal against a decision may be made only in respect of errors of law and not errors of fact. In extreme cases, a factual conclusion may be so perverse that it can be considered to be the result of an error of law and therefore subject to appeal.

Case: *Edwards (HM Inspector of Taxes) v Bairstow & Harrison* (1955) 36 TC 207

9.6.2   Error of law

An error of law will occur if the tribunal wrongly identifies the correct legal principles or applies an incorrect meaning of a statutory word. For example, a conclusion on whether there is deliberate conduct will ordinarily be a question of fact (and not susceptible to further challenge). However, if the tribunal had not considered the correct meaning of "deliberate", then an error of law would have occurred.

9.6.3   Error of fact

Errors of fact are not limited to what are known as primary facts, such as the date on which a certain event occurred. They can extend to evaluative and qualitative matters, for example whether (given the findings of primary fact) the taxpayer was careless.

In *Hannah*, the Upper Tribunal considered that a decision on staleness involved an evaluation of facts by the FTT. Accordingly, absent any error of approach, the Upper Tribunal was unable to intervene. Of course, given the Supreme Court's subsequent decision in *Tooth*, any finding that an assessment is invalid because the underlying discovery had gone stale would itself amount to an error of law and therefore would be something that the Upper Tribunal could deal with.

The same principle is undoubtedly engaged when it comes to any determination regarding careless or deliberate conduct.

Arguably, the application of the hypothetical officer test involves a binary question – was there or was there not enough information to alert the hypothetical officer to the potential under-assessment – which must be answered yes or no. However, in *Hannah* the Upper Tribunal considered that the question too was an evaluative one and therefore, absent any misdirection of law, it was not open to the Upper Tribunal to interfere with the decision.

Case: *Hannah v HMRC* [2021] UKUT 22 (TCC)

10. Consequential claims by taxpayers

10.1 Overview

The legislation here is far from clear. However, the author understands the position to be as follows:

- Where a discovery assessment newly gives rise to an opportunity to make a claim (or to increase the scope of an existing claim), such a claim may generally be made by the end of the tax year following that in which the assessment was made.

- This is, in general, extended to cover claims more generally, most elections and also applications or notices made by the end of the tax year following that in which the assessment was made.

- However, excluded from this extension are late claims, elections, applications and notices in cases where the discovery assessment was made to recover tax previously underpaid due to careless or deliberate conduct by the taxpayer or a person acting on the taxpayer's behalf.

- Nevertheless, where a discovery assessment has been made to recover tax previously underpaid due to careless or deliberate conduct, the taxpayer may still obtain the benefit of any claim or application provided that it is made within the normal time limits.

10.2 Introduction

10.2.1 Purpose of the special rules

The clear purpose of a discovery assessment is to enable HMRC to collect tax that should have been assessed at an earlier date but (for whatever reason) was not. In many cases, had the tax been assessed at that earlier date, it would have been possible for the taxpayer to mitigate the liability by making a timely claim for relief or an election.

However, by the time a discovery assessment is made, the normal time limits for making such a claim may well have passed. The statute therefore permits, in specified circumstances, late claims to be made so as to allow some reduction in (or even elimination of) the tax being charged by the assessment.

10.2.2   Potential difficulties with the special rules

The special rules are not a panacea as they do not cover all situations. Furthermore, the rules are badly written and susceptible to different interpretations. To make matters worse (or perhaps better), HMRC's own published guidance appears to be at odds with the one aspect of the rules that appears to be relatively clear – HMRC's interpretation being far more generous than the author would consider appropriate.

A further difficulty is that many of the provisions were enacted without any discussion in Parliament, and so the original intention of the rules is even harder to discern.

Finally, there is currently a dearth of case law to shed light on the provisions although this is a matter that might well change in the coming years.

10.3 Section 43(2)

10.3.1   Overview

Of the special rules, s. 43(2) is the oldest and predates the 1970 Act itself.

Section 43 itself deals with time limits for claims. Section 43(1) provides an overriding four-year time limit (previously six years) whenever the statute does not provide otherwise.

Section 43(2) permits later claims to be made if an assessment has been made. When s. 43(2) applies, the claim "may be made at any time before the end of the [tax] year … following that in which the assessment was made".

Example

Alison is subject to a discovery assessment in relation to the 2018-19 tax year. It was made on 2 May 2024. Alison now wishes to make a claim for relief, for which the normal four-year time limit applies.

The normal time limit provides that Alison should have made the claim by 5 April 2023. However, if s. 43(2) applies (for which see **10.3.2** below), the claim may now be made any time up to the end of the tax year after that in which the assessment was made, i.e. by 5 April 2026.

Law: TMA 1970, s. 43

10.3.2   When does section 43(2) apply?

Section 43(2) applies to a claim "which could not have been allowed but for the making of an assessment".

What is not immediately clear is when the statutory words are supposed to be relevant. The most obvious difficulty is that claims are not routinely "allowed"; in particular, how can the prior making of an assessment be the event that causes a claim to be allowed?

It is the author's view that the legislation is concerned with a situation in which income (or a capital gain) is newly brought into charge, therefore newly giving rise to a need or opportunity for a claim for relief to be made.

Example 1

Liam is self-employed. His self-assessment for 2019-20 shows trading losses and no tax to pay. Following an investigation, HMRC disallow a trading expense. The adjustment causes a taxable profit of £25,000 to arise instead.

As Liam had made a trading loss in the subsequent year (2020-21), he seeks to set off that loss against the newly-assessed profit.

Such claims should ordinarily be made by 31 January in the second tax year following the loss-making year (31 January 2023). However, s. 43(2) extends this (if necessary) to the end of the tax year following that in which the discovery assessment is made.

Common sense would dictate that all consequential claims ought to be available in such circumstances. However, so far as s. 43(2) is concerned, this depends on the precise meaning of "could not have been allowed". Although this is not beyond doubt, the author is of the view that s. 43(2) applies only to claims that could not have been validly made but for the making of the assessment. This can be seen by comparing the situation of Liam in **Example 1** above with that of Lianne in **Example 2** below.

Example 2

Lianne is self-employed. Her self-assessment for 2022-23 shows trading losses and no tax to pay. Following an investigation which does not conclude until 2028, HMRC disallow a trading expense giving rise to a taxable profit of £25,000.

Thinking she had no tax to pay, Lianne decided not to claim any capital allowances in 2022-23. Now that tax is payable, Lianne wishes to mitigate the situation by making a late claim for capital allowances. For the sake of this example, the separate requirement for capital allowances claims to be made in a return is ignored.

Since a capital allowances claim could have been made even without the assessment (albeit with potentially little benefit), there is a real possibility that s. 43(2) cannot be used to extend the time limits.

The distinction (if it exists) is undoubtedly capricious. However, it is to some extent remedied by the provisions of s. 43A (see **10.4** below).

Law: TMA 1970, s. 43(2), 43A; ITA 2007, s. 64(5)

10.3.3 Supplementary claims

Section 43(2) applies both to new claims and also to claims which supplement those previously made.

Therefore, for example, a claim to carry back losses and to set them off against income of an earlier year can be extended by a supplementary claim if a discovery assessment increases the taxable profits of that earlier year.

For completeness, it should be noted that the corporation tax case of *Civic* could be cited as disproving the above. Equally, it could be said that s. 43(2) represents a key procedural difference between the income tax and corporation tax rules. Furthermore, the correctness of the court's decision in *Civic* is not universally accepted.

Law: TMA 1970, s. 43(2)

Case: *Civic Environmental Systems Ltd v HMRC* [2023] EWCA Civ 722

10.3.4   Other restrictions in section 43(2) cases

Section 43(2) applies only to claims. It does not apply to elections. Again, this restriction is somewhat softened by the provisions of s. 43A (discussed at **10.4** below).

10.4 Section 43A

10.4.1   Overview

The apparently capriciously restrictive nature of s. 43(2) is somewhat mitigated by the provisions of s. 43A which provide an extended period in which to make claims if a discovery assessment has been made.

Section 43A is subject to the limits set out in s. 43B (discussed at **10.4.8** and **10.4.9** below).

Law: TMA 1970, s. 43A

10.4.2   Scope of section 43A

Section 43A is not limited to claims. It applies to claims, elections, applications and notices, provided that they are "relevant".

Furthermore, any previously made claims, elections, applications and notices may be revoked or varied, provided again that they are "relevant".

The meaning of "relevant" is discussed at **10.4.6** below.

Law: TMA 1970, s. 43A(2)(a), (b)

10.4.3   Conditions for section 43A

The principal condition is that there is a discovery assessment which has been made otherwise than to make good a loss of tax caused by careless or deliberate conduct by the taxpayer or a person acting on the taxpayer's behalf. This is discussed further below.

However, the provisions add a further condition. This is that the relevant claim, election, application or notice "could have been made or given within the time allowed by the Taxes Acts". The meaning of this is once again unclear. However, the author interprets this as covering any case where the only bar to the claim (etc.) now being made is the fact that it is out of time. Provided the case comes within the scope of s. 43A then a new time limit arises giving at least a further year for the claim (etc.) to be made.

In a case involving the revocation or variation of a previous claim (etc.), the revocation or variation must be made in the same manner as the original claim (etc.). Furthermore, if it was subject to another person's consent, that same person (or, in the case of an individual who has since died, that individual's personal representatives) must give consent for the revocation or variation.

In addition, the extended time limit does not apply to revocations and variations if the previous claim was irrevocable (by virtue of a statutory provision).

Law: TMA 1970, s. 43A(2)(a), (b)

10.4.4 Section 43A disapplied in cases of careless or deliberate conduct

Section 43A does not apply, however, in cases where the assessment was made to reverse a tax loss brought about carelessly or deliberately by the taxpayer or a person acting on the taxpayer's behalf.

These tests are discussed more fully in **Chapter 5** above.

Law: TMA 1970, s. 43A(1)(b)

10.4.5 Extended time limit in section 43A cases

Where s. 43A applies, the time limit is extended to the end of the tax year following that in which the assessment is made.

This extension is the same as applicable in s. 43(2) cases. However, as discussed, s. 43A has a wider application than s. 43(2).

Law: TMA 1970, s. 43A(2)(a)

10.4.6 Relevant claims, elections, applications or notices

In the case of a claim for the recovery of overpaid tax (TMA 1970, Sch. 1AB), the claim is relevant if it relates to the same tax year as the discovery assessment.

Other claims, together with elections, applications and notices, are relevant if:

- they relate to the same tax year as the assessment; and
- making them (or, if appropriate, their revocation or variation) has or could have the effect of reducing any of the following:
  - the increased tax liability as a result of the assessment;
  - any other tax liability of the person concerned for the same tax year as that to which the assessment relates; or
  - any other tax liability of the person concerned for any tax year which follows that tax year provided that it ends within one year of the end of the tax year in which the assessment is made.

Example

On 15 March 2024, Isaac receives a discovery assessment in relation to the 2019-20 tax year.

If s. 43A applies, a late claim, election, application or notice may be made to reduce that assessment or any other tax liability that Isaac has in relation to any of the tax years from 2019-20 to 2024-25.

The cap on the relief as imposed by s. 43B(3) (see **10.4.8** below) should be noted, however.

Law: TMA 1970, s. 43A(2B), (3), (4)

Excluded elections

The statute provides that certain elections fall outside the definition of claim, election, application or notice. Effectively, such elections should be treated as not "relevant" for the purposes of the legislation.

These excluded elections are:

- elections made under ITA 2007, s. 47 to 49 (transfer of entitlement to a tax reduction between spouses and civil partners);
- elections made under ITA 2007, s. 55C (transfer of transferable tax allowance for married couples and civil partners); and

- elections under TCGA 1992, s. 35(5) (rebasing of assets to 31 March 1982 value).

Law: TMA 1970, s. 43A(2A)

10.4.7 *Giving effect to claims, elections, applications or notices*

The statute provides that all such adjustments shall be made as are required to take account of the effect that the claim, election, application or notice on any person's tax liability for any year of assessment.

Such adjustments may be made "by way of discharge or repayment of tax or the making of assessments or otherwise".

It is implicit that the rules permitting enquiries into claims (and repayments to be suspended for the duration of such enquiries) are not overridden.

Law: TMA 1970, s. 43A(5), Sch. 1A

10.4.8 *Limit on value of claims (etc.)*

A late claim, election, application and notice permitted by s. 43A may do no more than reduce the additional tax being charged by the assessment. It may not give rise to relief in excess of that.

As noted at **10.4.6** above, it is still possible to reduce tax liabilities in relation to other tax years. However, the total value of the relief is nevertheless restricted to the additional tax being charged by the assessment.

If this cap applies and the claim, election, application or notice affects more than one tax year and/or more than one person, then the reduction is to be apportioned:

- in the first instance, by an HMRC officer who must give written notice of the apportionment to each person affected; but
- this can be overridden by an apportionment being made by the taxpayer (or, if relevant, all the persons jointly) by written notice within 30 days of the officer's own notice of apportionment.

Law: TMA 1970, s. 43B(3), (4), (5)

10.4.9 Impact on third parties

If the late claim, election, application or notice would affect the tax liability of another person, that other person (or, in the case of an individual who has died, his or her personal representatives) must consent in writing to the late claim (etc.).

That other person may not make a further claim, election, application or notice by virtue of s. 43A to mitigate against any additional liability that arises.

Law: TMA 1970, s. 43B(1), (2)

10.5 Section 36(3)

10.5.1 Overview

The most restrictive special rule is found in TMA 1970, s. 36(3) and deals with cases where a discovery assessment is made and the loss of income tax or CGT was:

- brought about carelessly by the taxpayer or a person acting on the taxpayer's behalf;
- brought about deliberately by the taxpayer or a person acting on the taxpayer's behalf;
- attributable to a failure by the taxpayer to notify HMRC of the taxpayer's chargeability to tax;
- attributable to arrangements in respect of which the taxpayer has failed to comply with a DOTAS obligation under FA 2004, s. 309, 310 or 313; or
- attributable to arrangements which were expected to give rise to a tax advantage in which the taxpayer was under a disclosure obligation under FA 2014, s. 253 (POTAS) but failed to make such a disclosure.

These circumstances are those in which HMRC may make discovery assessments more than the usual four years after the tax year to which the assessment relates (and indeed up to 20 years afterwards) (see **8.2.4** above). It should be noted, however, that s. 36(3) can nevertheless apply even if the discovery assessment is made within the usual four-year period.

Law: TMA 1970, s. 36(3)

10.5.2   Effect of s. 36(3)

It is the author's view that s. 36(3) does not permit any late claims or applications to be newly made.

Accordingly, however, if a claim or application had already been made within the statutory time limits, the taxpayer may request that relief be given to reflect such a claim or application to mitigate the effect of a discovery assessment.

It should be noted that the tribunal has made brief reference to this provision in the case of *Dugan* and gave it a different interpretation. In particular, the tribunal took the view that s. 36(3) can apply to claims made *after* the discovery assessment. As the tribunal noted:

> "we do not read s 36(3) as requiring that the claim be made before the making of the assessment – that would be perverse".

However, it is respectfully considered that the tribunal was approaching the section from the wrong direction and that, given the previous finding of carelessness, should have recognised the restrictions on the making of consequential claims.

Law: TMA 1970, s. 36(3)

Case: *Dugan v HMRC* [2016] UKFTT 618 (TC)

10.5.3   Possible extension to most elections

Given that the legislation refers only to "a claim or application" (whereas s. 43A, which was introduced at the same time, refers to claims, elections, applications or notices) it would appear that s. 36(3) would not cover elections. This is the position taken by HMRC in their manuals at CH 55200 and SACM 9010.

There again, statute has been further amended by the subsequent and express exclusion of a specific type of election being those made under ITA 2007, s. 47 to 49 (transfer of entitlement to a tax reduction between spouses and civil partners).

Example

Angelique (born in 1930) and her civil partner (Noreen) made a joint election under ITA 2007, s. 48 permitting Angelique to claim the full amount of the married couple's allowance.

She is subsequently assessed for income that has been carelessly omitted from her tax return.

Angelique is not entitled to have the benefit of her joint election taken into account in respect of the amount payable under the discovery assessment.

Law: TMA 1970, s. 36(3A)
Guidance: CH 55200; SACM 9010

10.5.4 HMRC give s. 36(3) a wider effect

HMRC's practice, however, is to treat s. 36(3) as if it does in fact permit late claims (but not elections) to be made even in cases where there has been careless or deliberate conduct.

The guidance manual makes it clear that not all claims may be made late under s. 36(3), and it specifically lists (as those excluded from the section) claims for negligible value (TCGA 1992, s. 24(2)) and claims for relief on the irrecoverability of a loan made to a trader (TCGA 1992, s. 253).

Care should be taken before relying on this guidance, however. In particular, the specific exclusions referred to appear to have no statutory justification.

Guidance: SACM 9010

Holdover relief claims

Adding to the confusion is a restriction found in HMRC's capital gains manual in relation to holdover relief claims under TCGA 1992, s. 165. Noting the absence of an equivalent to the rule in s. 43A(5) (which permits adjustments to be made to other taxpayer's position), the manual suggests that this precludes holdover relief claims being made at all under s. 36(3). There seems to be no justification for such a limitation being imputed into the statute.

Whatever the correct interpretation, the same outcome would be likely to apply to holdover relief claims under s. 260.

Law: TMA 1970, s. 165, 260
Guidance: CG 66889

10.6 Exceptional cases where late claims might be permitted

10.6.1 Overview

There are other exceptional cases in which a late claim might be permitted under the statute. They are not specific to cases in which a discovery assessment (or perhaps an adjustment on a closure notice) has been made, although they may well be relevant in such cases.

10.6.2 Legislation permits a late claim

In some situations, the statute itself provides for an extended time limit. One clear example is the corporation tax group relief rules, which extend the time limits in certain specific situations.

Those specific situations do not extend to cases involving discovery assessments (partly because the statute caters for them as described above). However, there is a residual right for taxpayers to make a claim "at a later time if an officer of Revenue and Customs allows it".

Law: FA 1998, Sch. 18, para. 74(1), (2)
Guidance: *Statement of Practice* 5/01

10.6.3 Reasonable excuse for late claim

Typically, in cases involving penalties, taxpayers have relied upon the provisions of TMA, s. 118(2). That subsection provides that a time limit is not to be treated as missed provided that both:

- the taxpayer had a reasonable excuse for missing the time limit; and
- any failure is remedied without unreasonable delay once the reasonable excuse cease to apply.

In *Raftopoulou*, the Court of Appeal concluded that this provision applied only in cases where the taxpayer had a positive duty to take a particular action within the specified time (e.g. submit a tax return or make a particular payment). It did not apply to taxpayers who wished to take advantage of an option (e.g. make a claim).

Law: TMA 1970, s. 118(2)
Case: *HMRC v Raftopoulou v HMRC* [2018] EWCA Civ 818

10.6.4 Under HMRC's inherent powers

Even when the statute does not contain a specific power extending a time limit, the legislation governing the conduct of HMRC itself provides HMRC with the discretion to admit claims out of time.

This power was historically known as HMRC's care and management power but was rather crudely renamed "collection and management" in 2005, although its statutory meaning has been expressly preserved.

The leading case concerning its use is the Court of Appeal's decision in *Unilever*. (Although that was a case involving group relief, for which there is now a specific provision permitting late claims, there was no such provision at the time.)

HMRC have guidance explaining their approach to late claims. However, as shown in *Ames*, HMRC's adherence to their own guidance can sometimes be superficial.

Law: CRCA 2005, s. 5(1), 51(3)
Cases: *R v Inland Revenue Commissioners ex parte Unilever plc* (1996) 68 TC 205; *R (oao Ames) v HMRC* [2018] UKUT 190 TCC
Guidance: SACM 10040

10.6.5 Under human rights legislation

Finally, if a discovery assessment (when combined with an otherwise missed time limit) will lead to double taxation (the same income being taxed twice), the case of *Fessal* shows that a late claim might still be admitted.

Case: *Fessal v HMRC* [2016] UKFTT 285 (TC)

10.7 Corporation tax

10.7.1 Overview

The corporation tax rules take a similar approach and, in particular, distinguish between careless and deliberate conduct cases and those less culpable situations.

Law: FA 1998, Sch. 18, para. 61-65

10.7.2   Careless or deliberate cases

The key difference in corporation tax cases is that careless or deliberate conduct by a person who was, at the relevant time, a partner of the company is sufficient to exclude the company from the possibility of an extended time limit.

The term "relevant time" is not defined and is thought therefore to mean the time when the allegedly careless or deliberate conduct took place.

Law: FA 1998, Sch. 18, para. 61(2)(c), 65(1)(c)

10.7.3   The extended time limit

In corporation tax cases the extended time limit permits a claim, election, application or notice to be given at any time within one year of the end of the accounting period in which the discovery assessment is made.

Or, in the case of an irrevocable claim (etc.), such a claim (etc.) if previously made may be revoked or varied within one year of the end of the accounting period in which the discovery assessment is made.

Law: FA 1998, Sch. 18, para. 61(3)(b), 62(1)

10.7.4   Claims affecting more than one period

One further potential practical difference arises from the fact that self-assessment operates slightly differently from corporation tax self-assessment when claims affect more than one period.

In self-assessment cases, the claim is statutorily deemed to relate to the later year. There is no such deeming provision in relation to corporation tax. Therefore, the requirement that the claim relates to the period in respect of which the discovery assessment relates can have different consequences, depending on the taxes involved.

The *Civic* case should also be noted, although its correctness is not universally accepted. In that case, a company's profits for year 1 were eliminated by a carry-back claim in respect of year 2's losses. When HMRC successfully increased the profits for year 1, they refused to allow the surplus losses from year 2 to be set off against the increased profits. The Court of Appeal held that HMRC were correct. In that case, the year 1 adjustments were made by closure notice and not a discovery assessment. It is unclear to what extent that distinction is material.

Law: TMA 1970, Sch. 1B, para. 2(3), 3(2), 4(2), 5(2); FA 1998, Sch. 18, para. 62(2)(a)

Case: *Civic Environmental Systems Ltd v HMRC* [2023] EWCA Civ 722

10.8 Other taxes

There are no provisions permitting a consequential claim to be made following a discovery assessment in relation to the following taxes:

- SDLT;
- ATED;
- digital services tax;
- public interest business protection tax; and
- multinational top-up tax.

11. Interaction between discovery assessments and investigatory powers

11.1 Enquiries

It is a fundamental aspect of self-assessment that HMRC have enquiry powers and that those powers entitle HMRC to make reasonable requests for information. This is provided for by FA 2008, Sch. 36.

However, Sch. 36 then distinguishes between those investigations that are being conducted in the course of a statutory enquiry and those outside the framework of such an enquiry.

This chapter provides a brief overview of the interaction of the Sch. 36 provisions and the discovery assessment rules.

For a fuller discussion of HMRC's information powers under Sch. 36, see the author's *Schedule 36 Notices*, from Claritax Books.

Law: FA 2008, Sch. 36, para. 21(4)

11.2 Investigations outside statutory enquiries

11.2.1 Scope of HMRC's information powers

The general rule governing HMRC's information requests is that the information must be "reasonably required" for the purposes of checking the taxpayer's tax position (or in relation to enforcing a tax debt). That general rule is, in essence, the only restriction on what HMRC may ask for in the course of a statutory enquiry.

Outside a statutory enquiry, however, HMRC have more limited powers.

Law: FA 2008, Sch. 36, para. 1(1)

PAYE cases

Under FA 2008, Sch. 36, HMRC can request information reasonably required for the purposes of checking PAYE compliance.

Law: FA 2008, Sch. 36, para. 21(8)

Cases involving other taxes

Under FA 2008, Sch. 36, HMRC can also request information reasonably required for the purposes of checking compliance with taxes other than the main self-assessed taxes (i.e. taxes other than income tax, CGT and corporation tax).

Law: FA 2008, Sch. 36, para. 21(7)

Cases which might lead to a discovery assessment

Furthermore (and specifically in the context of income tax, CGT and corporation tax), HMRC may justify an information request in cases where the information might lead to a discovery assessment. This is considered further below.

Law: FA 2008, Sch. 36, para. 21(6)

11.2.2 Restrictions on information powers in potential discovery cases

Statutory restrictions

Under the statute, HMRC can justify an information notice if they can show that they have reason to suspect that the information (once provided) would lead to a discovery.

In *Betts*, the information notice was set aside by the FTT because there was insufficient evidence provided by HMRC to show a reason to suspect underpayment. That was a case in which the taxpayer had claimed to have become non-resident: a claim which HMRC belatedly wished to investigate. HMRC could demonstrate to the FTT why they were interested in investigating the taxpayer (i.e. there would be additional tax to pay if he were found to have remained UK-resident). However, a mere reason to be interested was not enough to overcome the hurdle in the legislation.

Law: FA 2008, Sch. 36, para. 21(6)
Case: *Betts v HMRC* [2013] UKFTT 430 (TC)

Restrictions found in case law

From a practical perspective, however, it seems rather unsatisfactory if HMRC need only show that they have reason to suspect an under-assessment.

For an extreme example, suppose that HMRC think that there has been an under-assessment in a tax return submitted 15 years earlier but that there is no reason to believe that the under-assessment was attributable to deliberate conduct (or any of the other circumstances justifying a 20-year time limit). In such cases, it might well be the case that HMRC can prove a discovery and they might also be able to show that there has definitely been an under-assessment. However, unless HMRC can also show deliberate conduct (to extend the statutory time limit to 20 years), any assessment made will be invalid. For these reasons, it would be unreasonable to require a taxpayer to provide information if there is little chance of it leading to a valid discovery assessment.

This point was recognised (in the context of HMRC's former information seeking powers) by the High Court in *Johnson*. The *Johnson* approach was subsequently applied by the Court of Session in *Pattullo*. (It should be noted that in *Pattullo*, the Court of Session considered the likely success of an argument based on s. 29(5), but that the approach adopted by the Court of Session has been superseded by later case law. See **Chapter 6** above for the up-to-date case law.)

It is understood that HMRC accept that this further restriction is applicable under Sch. 36 as it was to the former TMA 1970, s. 20 powers and this is reflected in HMRC's guidance.

This has since been confirmed by the FTT in the *Hegarty* case. There the tribunal remarked that either:

- one had to infer this additional restriction into the statute; or
- it was a part of the "reasonably required" test.

Cases: *R (oao Johnson) v Branigan* [2006] EWHC 885 (Admin); *Petition of Pattullo* [2009] CSOH 137; *Hegarty v HMRC* [2018] UKFTT 774 (TC)
Guidance: CH 23526

11.3 Other taxes

The equivalent rules for other taxes can found as follows:

- non-resident CGT: FA 2008, Sch. 36, para. 21ZA(5);
- SDLT: FA 2008, Sch. 36, para. 21A(5); and
- ATED: FA 2008, Sch. 36, para. 21B(5).

There is no express provision in relation to the digital services tax, the public interest business protection tax or the multinational top-up tax.

Appendix 1 – Statement of Practice 8 (1991) (Annotated)

General

1. This Statement of Practice explains, in relation to Income Tax, Corporation Tax and Capital Gains Tax, the circumstances in which HM Revenue and Customs (HMRC) seek to recover tax when a person has not been assessed or has been inadequately assessed. The statement does not cover cases where there may have been fraud or negligence by or on behalf of the taxpayer.

    There is no reason to think that HMRC's approach is likely to be different in relation to SDLT or ATED which have been introduced in more recent years.

2. The statement draws attention to the relevant statute and case law, in particular to the cases of:

    - *Cenlon Finance Co Ltd v Ellwood* ((1962) AC 782)
    - *Scorer v Olin Energy Systems Ltd* ((1985) BTC 181)

    Those cases are discussed at 3.3.3 and 3.9.2 above (Cenlon) and 3.4.2 above (Olin).

3. The following paragraphs should be read as subject to the general proviso that it is fundamental to the operation of the tax system that it is for the taxpayer, who is in possession of the facts, to supply them to HMRC so that his tax liability may be determined. Case law confirms that, if the relevant facts have not been accurately, fully and clearly disclosed by the taxpayer at the time, HMRC should not regard agreements reached, or action taken or omitted by its officials as binding it to accept less than the full amount of tax legally due.

4. This statement of practice applies to the following for the years specified:

    - individuals – for returns for years to and including 1995 to 1996

- partnerships whose trade, profession (or) business (was) set up and commenced before 6 April 1994 – for returns for the years to and including 1996 to 1997

- for bodies within the charge to Corporation Tax – for accounting periods ending before 1 July 1999

- for periods after those referred to above, Taxes Management Act (TMA) 1970 s 29, as amended by Finance Act (FA) 1994 ss 191, applies, except for companies. In the case of companies FA 1998 Sch 18 paras 41 to 45 apply

This is a very long way of saying that the Statement of Practice will govern cases within self-assessment as well as those from earlier years.

Inspectors' discovery powers

5.   TMA 1970 s 29(3) (old version) provides that where, after an assessment has been made or a decision has been taken that an assessment is not required, an inspector discovers that any taxable profits have not been assessed, he may make an assessment in the amount he considers ought to be charged. Similarly, a further assessment may be made if an inspector discovers that an assessment is insufficient or that a relief should be withdrawn. These powers may also be exercised by the Commissioners for HMRC. There are also other discovery provisions in the Taxes Acts which empower an inspector to make assessments to recover excessive reliefs, tax unpaid and over-repayments of tax, for example TMA 1970 s 30 and *Income and Corporation Taxes Act* 1988 ss 252, 412(3). Normally any assessment or further assessment must be made not later than 6 years after the end of the chargeable period to which it relates (TMA 1970 s 34(1)).

Former section 29(3) is now section 29(1).

The time limit is now generally four years (see 8.2.1 above).

6.   The courts have established that, subject to the decisions in the *Cenlon* and *Olin* cases, a change of opinion can amount to 'discovery'; that discovery can be made by an inspector other than the one who made the first assessment; and that discovery

can extend to a finding that the law has been incorrectly applied as well as the coming to light of additional facts. The word has been held to include any situation in which for any reason it newly appears to an inspector that a taxpayer has been undercharged.

This is agreed (see 3.3.3 above).

The main principles

7.   Two main principles are relevant in considering whether a discovery assessment may be made in any particular circumstances.

First, HMRC do not go back on a specific agreement made by an inspector on a particular point and raise a discovery assessment in respect of that point, whether or not the inspector correctly took account of current law and practice in entering into that agreement.

They sometimes do. But they should not.

Second, in circumstances where it cannot be said that the particular point was the subject of a specific agreement, HMRC regards itself as bound by the inspector's acceptance of a computation if the view of the point implicit in the computation was a tenable one.

But HMRC does not regard itself as bound by any agreement made, or considered to be made, or any decision taken by an inspector, if any of the information supplied on which that agreement or decision was founded was misleading.

The position in more detail

(i)   Specific agreement: appeal cases

Cenlon

8.   First, there is the case where there has been a specific agreement made by an inspector on a particular point, ie, where an issue has been raised expressly by the inspector, the taxpayer or his agent (whether orally or in writing) and agreement has been reached on the treatment of that issue for tax purposes. The decision in the *Cenlon* case established that,

if an assessment has been determined on appeal in accordance with TMA 1970 s 54, a discovery assessment should not be made in respect of any particular point which had been specifically dealt with in the course of the determination of that appeal.

This is agreed (see 3.9.2 above).

Olin

9. The decision in the *Olin* case gives guidance on deciding whether (in the absence of express words making the position clear) a particular point has been agreed, or could be said to have been agreed, in the course of reaching an overall agreement on a person's tax liability for a particular period. The *Olin* case makes it clear that a particular point agreed may not only be an issue raised expressly by the inspector, the taxpayer, or his agent (whether orally or in writing), but also any point which was fundamental to the whole basis of the computation of the taxpayer's liability, and so clearly and fully described in the accounts or computations that its significance for the computation of the taxpayer's liability was clearly and immediately apparent. In these circumstances the inspector could not reasonably be regarded as having agreed the computation without having appreciated and accepted the point. In other words the inspector must have been clearly put on notice of the point.

    This is a rather optimistic interpretation of what was decided in the House of Lords. Their Lordships were at pains to emphasise that an agreement was reached by the officer "and it is of no consequence why". The only caveat included was that the agreement should not have been reached "due to misleading information".

10. The question whether a particular point is fundamental to the whole basis of the computation of the liability is one which must depend for its answer on the facts and circumstances of the particular case. At one extreme, there will be cases like *Olin* itself where the claim to set off the losses of the defunct trade against the profits of the continuing trade was fundamental in that it had a major impact on the computation of the liability

and, moreover, was so clearly and fully described in the computations that the inspector must have appreciated what was being claimed. In the House of Lords, Lord Keith concluded that the inspector's agreement to the computations would have led a reasonable man to believe that the inspector had decided to admit the claim. In circumstances like these, HMRC would accept that the particular point was covered by the agreement reached and could not subsequently be the subject of a discovery assessment.

The introduction of a further test of what constitutes a "fundamental point" is an HMRC invention.

11.   At the other extreme, there will be cases in which a point is not fundamental to the basis of the computation, in that it does not have a major impact on the liability, or it is not so clearly and fully described in the accounts or computations that its significance is clearly and immediately apparent from the information supplied. For example, in cases where the taxpayer or his agent are claiming a particular deduction in arriving at profits, and among a multiplicity of items contained in the accounts and supporting material is a piece of information which, if the inspector had studied it in detail and thought through the implications, could have alerted him to the fact that the claim was not valid, HMRC would not accept that a discovery assessment could not be raised in respect of the particular (incorrect) deduction. Moreover, if further information were needed before the inspector could reasonably be expected to appreciate the significance of the point for the taxpayer's liability, HMRC would not accept that the inspector should be regarded as having considered and agreed that point.

As noted above, the introduction of a further test of what constitutes a "fundamental point" is an HMRC invention.

12.   The treatment of cases in between these 2 extremes must be a matter of judgment, depending on the particular facts. It will be necessary to decide, taking a reasonable and commonsense view of the matter, whether a taxpayer or his adviser would consider that a competent inspector, in examining the accounts and computations, must be considered to have addressed his

mind to the point at issue before signifying his agreement to the computation of the liability. This will be so only if the point was both fundamental to the whole basis of the computation, and was so clearly and fully described that its significance for the computation of the taxpayer's liability was clearly and immediately apparent. In these circumstances the inspector could not reasonably be regarded as having agreed the computation without having appreciated and accepted the point.

As noted above, the introduction of a further test of what constitutes a "fundamental point" is an HMRC invention.

(ii) Specific agreement: non-appeal cases

13. The principles established in the *Cenlon* and *Olin* cases strictly apply only where there was an appeal against an assessment or an appeal against a decision on a claim given in accordance with TMA 1970 s 42 which was subsequently determined either by the Commissioners or under TMA 1970 s 54. But, even if there was no determination of an appeal, a discovery assessment will not be made if the particular point on which the inspector takes a revised view was, or (as in the *Olin* case, see para 9 above) could be said to have been, the subject of the specific agreement of the final figures for assessment purposes. These circumstances may arise because the figures were agreed before an assessment was made, because the inspector decided not to make an assessment, or because the inspector's decision on the claim was accepted.

This is supported by the more recent Easinghall case (see 3.4.2 above).

(iii) No specific agreement: appeal and non-appeal cases

14. There will also be circumstances in which the *Cenlon* and *Olin* principles are not applicable. Thus, the particular point on which the inspector subsequently takes a revised view and considers making a discovery assessment may not have been the subject of a specific agreement or, because the point was not fundamental, cannot be said to have been the subject of a specific agreement (see para 8 above). In these circumstances, a discovery assessment will not be made, provided that the

inspector's original decision, whether on a claim or on the proper amount of an assessment, was based on a full and accurate disclosure of all the relevant facts and was a tenable view, so that the taxpayer could reasonably have believed that the inspector's decision was correct. And it follows that if the inspector's original decision was consistent with a view of the law and practice generally received or adopted at the time, a discovery assessment would not be made where, for example, there is a subsequent change in that practice – eg, following a court decision.

This was the birth of the rules which later became TMA 1970, s. 29(2) and (5).

Some particular circumstances where discovery assessments will be made

15.   The application in any individual case of the general principles described in the preceding paragraphs will, of course, depend on the particular facts and circumstances. But there are certain specific circumstances in which there will clearly be no grounds for an inspector not to make a discovery assessment, ie, where:

  - profits or income have not earlier been charged to tax because of any form of fraudulent or negligent conduct

  - the inspector has been misled or misinformed in any way about the particular matter at issue

  - there is an arithmetical error in a computation which had not been spotted at the time agreement was reached, and which can be corrected by the making of an in date discovery assessment

an error is made in accounts and computations which it cannot reasonably be alleged was correct or intended, eg, the double deduction from taxable profits of a particular item (say group relief).

Appendix 2 – Statement of Practice 1 (2006) (Annotated)

Overview

Self Assessment tax returns are usually issued to taxpayers in April, shortly after the end of the tax year. The Return has to be completed and sent in by the following 31 January. HM Revenue and Customs (HMRC) can open an enquiry into that return within 12 months of 31 January to check that the self assessment returns the right amount of tax. If it is incorrect the self assessment can be corrected:

> ***These dates do not relate to corporation tax, ATED or SDLT. However, there is no reason to think that HMRC's approach is likely to be different in relation to those other taxes. Indeed, it is confirmed below that the approach is adopted in corporation tax cases.***

There are some circumstances in which the tax inspector can assess further tax after the 12 month enquiry period. This usually happens when tax was under assessed because of fraud or negligence by the taxpayer but it can also happen if the taxpayer does not provide enough information for the inspector to realise, within the enquiry period, that the self assessment is insufficient:

> ***The terminology "fraud or negligence" should now be read as "careless or deliberate conduct".***

The judgment of the Court of Appeal in the case of *Langham v Veltema* was concerned with how much information the taxpayer needs to provide to remove the possibility of the inspector making a further assessment, known as a discovery assessment.

This Statement of Practice clarifies the circumstances in which HMRC seeks to recover tax when a self assessment is found to be insufficient after:

- the end of the period in which a notice of enquiry may be given
- an enquiry into a return has been completed

and it is considered that the information provided by the taxpayer was not sufficient to make the inspector aware of the insufficiency. The following examples illustrate what information taxpayers must disclose to guard against the possibility of a subsequent discovery assessment:

Therefore, it is clear that the guidance is relevant only to the question of insufficient disclosure (see Chapter 6 above). It provides no guidance in cases involving alleged carelessness or deliberate conduct.

Most taxpayers who use a valuation in completing their tax return and state in the Additional Information space at the end of the Return that a valuation has been used, by whom it has been carried out, and that it was carried out by a named independent and suitably qualified valuer if that was the case, on the appropriate basis, will be able, for all practical purposes, to rely on protection from a later discovery assessment, provided those statements are true:

As expanded upon below, the danger in over-reliance on this statement is HMRC's opening word "most".

Most taxpayers will be able to gain finality with exceptional items in accounts. An example might be a deduction in the accounts under Repairs. If an entry in the Additional Information space points out that a programme of work has been carried out that included repairs, improvements and new building work and that the total cost has been allocated to revenue and capital on a particular basis, the inspector should not enquire after the closure of the enquiry period unless he becomes aware that the statement was patently untrue or unreasonable:

Again, the danger in over-reliance on this statement is HMRC's opening word "most".

Taxpayers who adopt a different view of the law from that published as the HMRC view can protect against a discovery assessment after the enquiry period. The Return would have to indicate that a different view had been adopted by entering in the Additional Information space comments to the effect that they have not followed HMRC guidance on the issue or that no adjustment has been made to take account of it:

Of course, any such statement ought to be sufficient to preclude a discovery assessment. However, the subsequent case law demonstrates that such a statement is not necessary.

This statement does not cover cases where a self assessment is insufficient due to fraudulent or negligent conduct by or on behalf of the taxpayer:

The terminology "fraudulent or negligent conduct" should now be read as "careless or deliberate conduct".

This statement applies to the two main areas of self assessment:

- Income Tax and Capital Gains Tax
- Corporation Tax

ATED did not exist when the guidance was published.

In the case of SDLT, the standard return does not permit additional disclosures, although there is nothing to stop HMRC from applying the same principles in relation to other sources of information deemed to be before the hypothetical officer.

This statement of practice applies to the following for the years specified:

individuals – for returns from 1996 to 1997:

- partnerships – for returns from 1996 to 1997
- for bodies within the charge to Corporation Tax – accounting periods ending on or after 1 July 1999

Background

1. Prior to the introduction of Self Assessment, discovery assessments were subject to statute, case law and practice. Cases of particular relevance were *Cenlon Finance Co Ltd v Ellwood* 40 TC 176 and *Scorer v Olin Energy Systems Ltd* (1985). Statement of Practice 8 (1991) explained how the provisions were applied.

See Appendix 1 above.

2. When Income Tax Self Assessment (ITSA) was introduced by *Finance Act* (FA) 1994, new *Taxes Management Act* (TMA) 1970 s 29 was intended to reproduce the mix of law and practice on discovery set out in Statement of Practice 8 (1991). The Self Assessment Legal Framework issued in 1995 explained that the redrafting of TMA 1970 s 29 was to ensure:

    > "that a taxpayer who has made a full disclosure in the return has absolute finality 12 months after the filing date. This will be the case if the return is subsequently found to be incorrect, unless it was incorrect because of fraudulent or negligent conduct. In any case where there was incomplete disclosure or fraudulent or negligent conduct HMRC will still have the power to remedy any loss of tax".

    The intention was to offer finality, but there was also a recognition that there would be circumstances, even without fraud or neglect, that could still result in a discovery assessment. The equivalent legislation for Corporation Tax Self Assessment (CTSA) is at FA 1998, Sch. 18 para. 41 to 49.

    The various references to "fraudulent or negligent conduct" and "fraud and neglect" should now be read as if they read "careless or deliberate conduct".

3. The Court of Appeal in the case of *Langham (Ins of Taxes) v Veltema* [2004] STC 544, [2004] BTC 156, considered when disclosure was incomplete. It concluded that information made available, as defined in statute, must make an Inspector aware of an actual insufficiency in the assessment for that information to be complete enough to prevent the making of a discovery assessment. That conclusion gave rise to 2 concerns:

    *   the lack of finality for the taxpayer at the close of the enquiry window
    *   the inherent difficulty of complying with the law as expounded in the Court of Appeal

    This explains why HMRC subsequently issued this guidance.

4. Guidance was issued in December 2004 to help ITSA taxpayers achieve finality when completing their 2004 returns. This

Statement of Practice confirms the position in respect of ITSA and extends it to CTSA. The circumstances in which HMRC will regard a taxpayer as having made a full disclosure are set out and assurance of finality is given in particular situations.

As noted above, there is no reason why HMRC would not apply a similar approach in cases involving SDLT and ATED.

Discovery powers

5. The authority to make a discovery assessment is given by TMA 1970 s 29 (ITSA), FA 1998 Sch 19 para 41 (CTSA). In all cases, the relevant requirement for the purposes of this statement is a discovery 'that an assessment to tax is or has become insufficient'. Mere suspicion that an assessment may be insufficient is not adequate grounds for making a discovery assessment.

    The reference to Schedule 19 of FA 1998 should in fact be to Schedule 18. That aside, this is broadly correct. See 3.3.4 above.

6. Where there has not been fraudulent or negligent conduct, discovery can only take place where HMRC 'could not have been reasonably expected, on the basis of information made available before that time, to be aware of' the insufficiency in the assessment (TMA 1970 s 29(5); FA 1998 Sch 19 para 44(1)).

    But for the need to update the terminology to "careless or deliberate conduct", and for another incorrect reference to Schedule 19, this is broadly correct. See Chapter 5 above.

7. 'Information made available' is defined at TMA 1970 s 29(6) (ITSA), FA 1998 Sch 18 para 44(2) (CTSA). Relevant information includes that contained in documents accompanying the return.

    There are, of course, other sources of relevant information. See 6.5.3 above.

8. The requirement that HMRC must discover that an assessment is insufficient restricts the opportunity for using discovery powers to make an assessment. If HMRC consider that an assessment may be insufficient, it may seek more information

using TMA 1970 s 20 to establish whether the assessment is insufficient. However, where there is no reason to suspect fraud, the taxpayer will be told about the use of Section 20 and will have the opportunity to make representations to an independent Commissioner. The ability of HMRC to 'enquire' after the closure of the enquiry window is therefore subject to external oversight.

Since the repeal of TMA 1970, s. 20 and its replacement by FA 2008, Sch. 36, it is now easier for HMRC to obtain information with a view to a discovery assessment as prior judicial approval is no longer necessary. The reference to "an independent Commissioner" should now be understood as a reference to the FTT. Otherwise, the broad principle of this paragraph is correct. See 11.2.2 above.

Discovery in practice

9. A taxpayer can further restrict the opportunity for discovery by providing enough information for an HMRC officer to realise within the enquiry period that the self assessment is insufficient. However taxpayers are encouraged to submit the minimum necessary to make disclosure of an insufficiency. The *Veltema* judgment does not require the provision of enough information to quantify the effect on the assessment. Information will not be treated as being made available where the total amount supplied is so extensive that an officer 'could not have been reasonably expected to be aware' of the significance of particular information and the officer's attention has not been drawn to it by the taxpayer or taxpayer's representative.

This can be a useful paragraph to cite in disputes. Particularly since the Sanderson decision, there will be a tendency for taxpayers to err on the side of caution and provide lots of information. More importantly, HMRC are likely to say that the information provided was not sufficient and that a taxpayer should always have provided more. It is quite clear that HMRC do not wish (and do not expect) to be deluged with information in order to protect a taxpayer from a discovery assessment.

> *The idea that there is a concept of "too much information" is taken from the 1991 guidance (see Appendix 1 above), which mainly relates to the increasingly rare concept of whether a prior agreement precludes a subsequent discovery assessment (see 3.4.2 above). There is no case law to date as to whether it is correct in the context of the assumed knowledge of the hypothetical officer.*

10.   HMRC recognise that a taxpayer, unless acting fraudulently or negligently, will consider his return to be correct and complete with no insufficiency. Most figures entered on a return will be absolute, however some will be open to interpretation or uncertain. In these circumstances, the taxpayer will have made a judgment as to the correct figure to enter. HMRC may regard this figure as insufficient. Where the taxpayer has fully alerted HMRC to the full circumstances of such an entry on the return, then the HMRC officer is in a position to determine whether or not there is an insufficiency, the conditions set by the Court of Appeal in *Langham v Veltema* have been met and the assessment will not be open to discovery on that point.

The following examples illustrate common situations:

> *Of course, the real issue is what constitutes "fully alerted".*

Examples of common situations

Valuation cases

11.   Some entries on tax returns depend on the valuation of an asset. For example, if a company transfers a property to a director at less than market value, both the company and the director will need to use the market value in calculating the capital gain and benefit respectively. There is no obligation on the director to do any more than enter the resulting benefit in the relevant box on his return. However, the Court of Appeal decided in *Langham v Veltema* that the figure on the return does not give HMRC the level of information that is necessary to prevent a later discovery assessment.

> *This is not thought to be controversial.*

12.	Most taxpayers who state that a valuation has been used, by whom it has been carried out, and that it was carried out by a named independent and suitably qualified valuer if that was the case, on the appropriate basis, will be able, for all practical purposes, to rely on protection from a later discovery assessment, provided those statements are true.

This guidance initially appears to be providing some useful indications as to what taxpayers should include on their returns. The danger is that it is framed for the benefit of "most taxpayers". As will be seen below, it is impossible to know whether any individual taxpayer falls within the scope of the guidance or is in fact one of the exceptions.

13.	The main exception will be where, as in the example of a property transferred to a director, the same transaction is the subject of an agreed valuation in a related tax return, that of the company. It may then come to light that the director's return was insufficient and a discovery assessment raised. It is also likely that the insufficiency can be quantified without further enquiry. For this purpose, a related tax return is that of another party to the same transaction, rather than another transaction involving a similar or identical asset. The returns of several parties disposing of a jointly owned asset or shareholders disposing of all the shares in the same company in a single transaction, for example, may be related for this purpose.

Where taxpayers' interests in an asset or assets are similar, but not the same, any valuations agreed would not necessarily bind other taxpayers.

The guidance therefore carves out one category of taxpayer as being "the main exception". There is no indication as to the other categories of exception.

Furthermore, it will be seen that this "main exception" covers the scenario in which Mr Veltema found himself. Given that the guidance was published in order to clarify HMRC's view of the law in the wake of the Veltema case, this is quite unfortunate.

14. Information about the valuation may be provided in the Additional Information space (ITSA) or in accompanying documents (ITSA and CTSA). The return of capital gains for ITSA purposes requires an entry to indicate that a valuation has been used and asks for a copy of any valuation received. If these provide the information mentioned above the taxpayer can rely on protection from a later discovery assessment.

    Although not expressly stated, the guidance is alluding to the fact that HMRC do not need to be provided with a document for it to be deemed to be before the hypothetical officer. It is sufficient that the officer is able to infer its existence and relevance from other information deemed to be before him. See 6.5.3 above.

Other judgmental issues

15. There are many items such as reserves, provisions and stock valuation that are routinely included in accounts, as well as some exceptional items such as capital/revenue expenditure in repairs, which require an element of judgment on the part of the taxpayer or representative. Prior to the introduction of self assessment it was customary to provide details of such items in the accounts or computations and many taxpayers have continued to do so.

    As will become clear, HMRC do not suggest that this information should no longer be provided.

16. It is difficult to see how HMRC might come to the conclusion that an assessment is insufficient because of one of these items without making an enquiry. There will be instances in which it becomes clear from an in-year enquiry that previous years figures were incorrect. The decision in the *Veltema* case does not alter that situation.

    In other words, in order to prevent a discovery assessment, it is advisable for information to continue to be provided to HMRC with a return (or in one of the other ways of communicating with the hypothetical officer – see 6.5.3 above).

17.   It may be possible to gain finality with the more exceptional items. An example might be a deduction in the accounts under Repairs. If an entry in the Additional Information space or accompanying documentation points out that a programme of work has been carried out that included repairs, improvements and new building work and that the total cost has been allocated to revenue and capital on a particular basis, the HMRC officer will not use discovery powers after the closure of the enquiry period unless he becomes aware that the statement was patently untrue or the basis of allocation was so unreasonable as to be negligent.

It is hard these days to imagine that in such circumstances, "the HMRC officer will not use discovery powers". However, HMRC ought not to use the discovery powers in those circumstances and, in any event, the provision of the information should enable any discovery assessment to be defeated.

Taking a different view

18.   It is open to a taxpayer properly informed or advised to adopt a different view of the law from that published as HMRC's view. To protect against a discovery assessment after the enquiry period, the return or accompanying documents would have to indicate that a different view had been adopted. This might be done by comments to the effect that the taxpayer has not followed HMRC guidance on the issue or that no adjustment has been made to take account of it. This would offer an opportunity to HMRC to take up the return for enquiry. It is not necessary to provide all the documentation that HMRC might need to quantify that insufficiency if an enquiry into the return is made.

Of course, any such statement ought to be sufficient to preclude a discovery assessment. However, the subsequent case law demonstrates that such a statement is not necessary.

For example, in Swift, the tribunal considered that "an ordinary competent Inspector would have spotted the reference to "LLC" [on the return] and would have known of

HMRC's published view that no double taxation relief was available even without a specific reference to the fact that the Appellant was taking a different view".

Similarly, in Charlton, the Upper Tribunal said "We do not accept that there is any overriding requirement that the information has to explain how the scheme works ..., nor that the information must specify, if it be the case, that the view adopted by the taxpayer is different from that taken by HMRC".

Swift v HMRC [2010] UKFTT 88 (TC); HMRC v Charlton (and others) [2012] UKUT 770 (TCC).

19.   Provided the point at issue is clearly identified and the stance adopted is not wholly unreasonable, the existence of an under-assessment or insufficiency is demonstrated by the statement that a different view of the law has been followed. In these circumstances the taxpayer achieves finality if no enquiry is opened within the statutory time limit.

As shown in Swift and Charlton, a statement of the facts should be sufficient to alert the hypothetical officer to understand what HMRC's approach to the law would be and therefore to identify whether or not the taxpayer has adopted a different view.

Swift v HMRC [2010] UKFTT 88 (TC); HMRC v Charlton (and others) [2012] UKUT 770 (TCC).

Appendix 3 – Statutory instruments

The following UK statutory instruments are referred to in the text.

SI 2007/678	The Corporation Tax (Surrender of Terminal Losses on Films and Claims for Relief) Regulations 2007
SI 2009/403	The Finance Act 2008, Schedule 39 (Appointed Day, Transitional Provision and Savings) Order 2009
SI 2010/867	The Finance Act 2009, Schedule 51 (Time Limits for Assessments, Claims, etc.) (Appointed Days and Transitional Provisions) Order 2010
SI 2021/1079	The Finance (No. 2) Act 2017, Sections 60 and 61 and Schedule 14 (Digital Reporting and Record-Keeping) (Appointed Day) Regulations 2021

Table of primary legislation

211

Taxes Management Act 1970 (cont.)

Table of statutory instruments

(See **Appendix 3** for full names of SIs.)

Index of cases

221

General index